T0387316

INSIDE
LIVE
EVENTS

YOUR PLAYBOOK FOR
MASTERING THE EXPERIENCE

INSIDE
LIVE
EVENTS

Bob Priest-Heck &
Carrie Freeman Parsons

GREENLEAF
BOOK GROUP PRESS

Published by Greenleaf Book Group Press
Austin, Texas
www.gbgpress.com

Distributed by Greenleaf Book Group

For ordering information or special discounts for bulk purchases, please contact Greenleaf Book Group at PO Box 91869, Austin, TX 78709, 512.891.6100.

Design and composition by Greenleaf Book Group and Mimi Bark
Cover design by Greenleaf Book Group and Mimi Bark
Cover image used under license from ©Shutterstock.com/Fazakas Mihaly

Publisher's Cataloging-in-Publication data is available.

Print ISBN: 979-8-88645-261-7

eBook ISBN: 979-8-88645-262-4

To offset the number of trees consumed in the printing of our books, Greenleaf donates a portion of the proceeds from each printing to the Arbor Day Foundation. Greenleaf Book Group has replaced over 50,000 trees since 2007.

Printed in the United States of America on acid-free paper

24 25 26 27 28 29 30 31   10 9 8 7 6 5 4 3 2 1

First Edition

EVERY HUMAN ENDEAVOR comes wrapped in a paradox—the minute we commit to taking one course of action, we must also decide not to do many others. When we agreed to create a book about *how* live events are conceived and executed, we had to step away from the desire to write about *why* live events matter. That could fill several books, but the need for a comprehensive "how to" seemed more urgent. And frankly, people inside the event industry understand why events matter, even if we don't talk about it very often.

Maybe it's obvious, but for the rest of the world, it needs to be said: Live events are about bringing people together in a way that engenders commerce, learning, progress, innovation, and goodwill. History shows that live gatherings are essential to our humanity. Throughout history, people around the world have participated in ritual gatherings to mark marriages, funerals, military victories, and sacramental rites. The ancient Greek *agoras* supported lively markets but also served as places to discuss current events and ponder big issues. Professional societies flourished as the precursors to our trade associations, playing a huge role in curating, incubating, and broadcasting new ideas. People have always found ways to be together when something mattered. Why? Because sharing the experience makes it real.

We dedicate this book to all who have historically advanced this collective spirit. Merchants who displayed their wares in tents along the ancient trade routes. Nineteenth-century inventors who proposed breakthrough ideas to an incredulous exposition audience. Small entrepreneurs who bet everything on making it big at a national trade show.

We dedicate this book to the industry professionals who give their all, day after day, until the impossible seems routine.

We dedicate this book to the customers who have trusted us with their treasure—their brands, their loyal customers, their sustainable success.

And we dedicate this book to those who may not yet realize that this is the legacy they will build on, grow, and push into unimagined directions. Students, young professionals, and anyone who is dissatisfied with work that is predictable, isolating, and uninspired—we need you. The world needs you.

We have started this book in the hope that you will finish it.

Contents

PHASE 3: BUILD THE PLAN   171

PHASE 4: REVIEW AND IMPROVE   231

Introduction

We do events for a living. Freeman is one of the world's leading event companies, so we've seen firsthand the power of bringing people together to explore innovative ideas, grow businesses, advance education, improve the art and science of healing, and create memories that last forever. Events enable people to come together in synergistic ways. Our goal is to help make every gathering that connects people more meaningful.

WHO WE ARE

Bob Priest-Heck

I can't imagine a more fulfilling career than the one I've enjoyed in the events industry. I started out in hospitality at Hyatt, where I learned valuable lessons about human behavior and the need for empathetic leadership. That job brought me from the Midwest to California when the tech industry was emerging. I was brought in by Jonathan Seybold, who was turning hobby publishing into a technology–media powerhouse. We worked out of an old Malibu mansion next to Johnny Carson's home. That led to an opportunity to work with Dan Lynch to create environments and educate IT professionals on "network interoperability."

This initiated the adoption of TCP/IP protocols at events like Interop—basically creating the commercial internet infrastructure.

The debate about the future of the internet attracted people like Steve Jobs and Bill Gates, and our events gave them a forum to exchange and promote ideas. Eventually, I moved to Japan to spend several years building teams and disruptive technology events around the globe, creating brand experiences for emerging products and ascendant companies, leading to the launch of JavaOne in 1996. As breakthroughs in digital technology progressed, I consulted for different companies, envisioning a new breed of event agency.

When my path crossed with Freeman's, they invited me to join them and invested in making their vision a reality. I became the first non–family member to serve as Freeman's CEO, and I continue to serve on the board of directors. Today, my hope is that this book will help more people embrace and amplify the power of events to create positive change.

Carrie Freeman Parsons

In 1927, my grandfather Donald (Buck) Freeman decided to leverage his passion for organizing fraternity parties by founding an event-decorating business. Before long, the whole family was helping out with the new company. As a young boy, my father, Don Freeman Jr., started helping his sister pull staples out of old, wooden display tables. He later became company president in 1972 and was named chairman and CEO in 1977. Growing up, our family life was intertwined with the company, and I naturally saw the employees as extended family. I worked at the company in the summers and upon graduation in 1985 joined full time and fell in love with the possibilities. I realized that my family had created a culture based on shared values, mutual trust, and a keen sense of purpose, capable of building a vibrant, self-contained world where nothing had existed the day before and that would disappear the day after. We were part of an industry that touched every other sector of business, health care, sports, entertainment, education, and even social gatherings. By bringing people together, we were helping advance progress and prosperity. This reinforced my conviction that we can all "do well by doing good."

I've worked in a variety of offices and positions at Freeman, and I've been inspired by so many people in this industry, especially my father. In 2019, he became chair emeritus and named me chair. I'm proud and grateful to continue the family tradition. Every day, the people of Freeman strive to serve the community and harness our power to transform the world. I encourage anyone interested in creating meaningful change to join us.

WHY EVENTS MATTER

When people come together to share ideas, they can forever change the course of progress. The innovations, discoveries, and progressive ideas championed by visionaries and inventors over the centuries might never have flourished without the attention, influence, and collaboration of others. The meetings, trade shows, conferences, and exhibitions described in this book are hosted, designed, and produced by event creators working to connect people by creating a dedicated space for them to discover new synergies. Being part of this industry can feel exhausting, exhilarating, and deeply gratifying. It's hard work for event creators (our clients) and for us (the agencies and contractors responsible for bringing their vision to life). Yet, as challenging and overwhelming as the work sometimes seems, the results can be memorable and lasting. That's why we believe this work matters.

People in our industry cherish the thrill of being part of an event, whether it's a corporate extravaganza launching breakthrough technology or an association of high school teachers seeking new ways to reach kids. We're privileged to be part of something bigger than ourselves and to experience a unique sense of community, purpose, and shared passion. Events are experienced live, whether in person or streaming, so anything can happen. We can plan every detail and prepare for every contingency, but then we have to let go, hope for the best, and run interference as needed. While there's no guarantee that everything will go as planned, the work is never boring.

Not all events fulfill a high-minded purpose. Some serve purely as entertainment. Some throw parties to reward achievement. Some promote a brand or launch a new product. But we want to be part of these too because they can lift spirits, encourage progress, and enable prosperity. People leave better informed, better connected, and more confident than when they arrived. Sometimes, they change the world. That's our job, and it's a job that matters.

WHO SHOULD READ THIS BOOK

This book is for anyone who is curious about how concepts become real events that provoke positive action. Maybe you're an event planner, and you want to up your game. Maybe you're planning a special event and hope to pick up a few pointers. Maybe you're a specialist in experience marketing and interested in expanding your knowledge. Maybe you're looking for a career that keeps changing, growing, and challenging you in new ways.

IS A CAREER IN LIVE EVENTS RIGHT FOR YOU?

Are you the kind of person who dreads the tedium of repetitive nine-to-five office work? Do you like to travel? Do you enjoy fresh challenges and new opportunities? Then there may be no better employment for you. Event creation is a team sport. The sense of being part of a high-performing team, building interdependent relationships, and accomplishing amazing things together is what motivates us and keeps us going. This line of work enables you to meet interesting people and work with some of the finest, most resourceful professionals you can imagine. However, this work is not for everyone. Events happen on a rigid schedule, usually booked months or years in advance, and the on-site requirements are unforgiving. Weekend work, long hours, and short holidays are the norm. If you long for adventure and excitement, it could be the ideal career choice for you.

We know people from every academic background who have found meaningful careers in our industry: Creative people who struggled to feed their families in the theater world now make good livings as writers, directors, lighting and sound designers, stage managers, and producers of live events. High school graduates with some experience in drafting or carpentry are in high demand in fabrication shops. We know history majors who now manage corporate accounts and leaders who hated college but discovered they had a knack for thinking on their feet and staying calm in a crisis, making them perfectly suited for logistics work in managing load-in and load-out on the show floor. Architects enjoy the thrill of exhibit design, essentially building a small town in a few months and tearing it down again in three days. Programmers and tech workers weary of Silicon Valley use the latest innovations to support the people who attend the events we produce. Homebodies can provide phone support for exhibitors, while exhibitor services staff can travel to a new city every week.

Every type of traditional office job is still required to run the businesses that operate within the events industry. We hire accountants, lawyers, administrative assistants, human resources executives, training experts, and marketing and communications professionals—and they are all proud to be part of an industry that brings people together to make important things happen.

WHERE WE'RE COMING FROM

Creating an event requires a wide range of people, including the organization behind the event that employs staff to oversee it; the agencies, contractors, and suppliers who help them produce it; the exhibitors and sponsors who pay for their presence there; the audience who attends and participates; and the venues and hospitality partners who provide a place for the event to happen.

The variety of events is infinite, but as we discuss these unique experiences, we tend to speak in terms of a prototypical event. For example, many events include a meeting or conference, educational and networking opportunities, and an exposition or trade show. Associations or companies in the business of holding events typically host these shows, and the audience tends to consist of members of the hosting organization, its customers, or interested members of the public. Sponsors or exhibitors often participate so they can market to the event audience. Many corporations host their own internal events (for company meetings, team building, or product training) and exhibit at events in their business sector. These elements combine to characterize the prototypical event we tend to refer to in this book. Our goal is to demonstrate that the methodologies recommended here can be effective for any type of event. Every event should honor its obligation to the attendee and the host, which means meeting their needs while keeping an eye on the budget.

A STRATEGY FOR CONTINUOUS IMPROVEMENT

We've structured this book around a four-phase event methodology: 1) getting started, 2) designing the plan, 3) working the plan, and 4) reviewing and improving after the event wraps up. This process isn't magical, but we hope your results will be. For events held periodically, annually, or more frequently, this process is a continuous cycle. For shorter timelines, the phases may be compressed, but they still apply.

We base these four phases on a sensible foundation that includes these four concepts: 1) taking time to get the plan right before rushing ahead, 2) aligning your action plan against agreed-upon budgets and timelines, 3) doing things on purpose instead of just letting them happen, and 4) insisting that each new event improves upon what came before.

THE FOUR PHASES

 Phase 1: Get started. Build a multidisciplinary team. Articulate a strategic direction and ensure that everyone on your team agrees to pursue it. Build a strategy brief that lays out the specifics, assigns them success metrics, and drives your next steps. Imagine the event in detail, including every aspect of fulfilling the requirements of your strategy brief. Build an in-depth creative brief and implement a project-tracking system.

 Phase 2: Design the plan. Design the event from start to finish. Create an event budget, a production schedule, and a finalized timeline. Write an in-depth event plan, and make sure everyone approves it, as it will act as the blueprint for the professionals who actually execute the event.

 Phase 3: Build the plan. This includes what most people think of as "showtime," or going into production. This phase is where things get real—creating signage and exhibits, finalizing content, and building everything needed. "Everything" can be defined as your extensive list of deliverables, including the installation and execution of the event at the venue, followed by loading out (also known as *striking*) the event. This phase is the culmination of months of work—an exciting and challenging time.

 Phase 4: Review and improve. Celebrate the wins and recognize where you need to improve. A wrap event enables your team to participate in a debrief regarding key lessons learned, including budget reconciliation and other annotations to inform future events. File and share all documentation and other relevant materials so the next event starts from a place of seasoned insight.

HOW TO USE THIS BOOK

This book is designed to help readers find what they need, whether they read it cover to cover, dive straight to their area of interest, or consult it as a quick reference. As each phase is introduced, you'll find a summary of action items covered in that section. Each chapter in these four phases starts with a brief to-do list and features useful lists and helpful bulleted guides that are called out in gray boxes. For readers who are just thumbing through, this suggests an area to focus on. We've also included a feature labeled "Pro Tips," which offers strategic insights suggested by the experts we interviewed along the way. All of this content is designed to elevate your event planning and help ensure a memorable, effective experience for all participants. An index is provided at the back to help you jump directly to any specific topic.

THINKING LIKE A DESIGNER

Event design requires that everyone on the team think like a designer. This approach is foundational to every phase of the cycle and every execution within each phase. Simply put, *design thinking* means every team member should always be looking for ways to make the event better. Design thinking leads to design doing. Unless you're prepared to let things happen by accident, start off by designing a comprehensive event plan that addresses all the moving parts.

EVENT ORCHESTRATION

Approach the various aspects of an event the way a conductor leads an orchestra. The ideal event should lead participants on a journey, exploring different expressions of a unifying theme. A narrative provides a beginning, middle, and end to the experience, with motifs exploring different subthemes. Dynamic elements diversify the color, volume, mood, and expression. Ideally, every participant (whether attending virtually or in person) can become the hero of their own journey.

Personalization involves examining each aspect of the possible choices your attendees will make along the way. If you've designed the experience properly, attendees won't ever see the blood, sweat, and tears that went into making the event happen. They will just enjoy the journey, feeling empowered to consume content how and where they like. Enable personalized journeys by integrated technology like agenda planning tools, apps that help make the most of their time, and just-in-time choices that enhance their unique experiences in an intuitive, nonintrusive way.

A NOTE ON TIMING

This book focuses on the design and execution of a specific event but does not address the marketing and communication plans, which are necessary to any event. The scope of our methodology begins after the completion of foundational work, including vital arrangements regarding the event's concept, purpose, and dates (often nonnegotiable by the time our methodology kicks in). Our first phase begins after the decision to hold an event has been made and starts with the design decisions required to make the event successful.

ATTRACTING EXHIBITORS, PARTNERS, AND ATTENDEES

The extent of exhibitor marketing required to sell out an event show floor varies widely between events. Event sponsors are often happy to return to a large event with proven success. Brands pay for their presence at an event (signage, swag giveaways, promotions, exhibits, etc.), and event managers create marketing materials that demonstrate the value of an upcoming event offering (often the first "deliverable" required of the event team).

The event's marketing plan should also include strategies targeting different audiences with a discrete value-based message. Materials created to promote the event campaign involve some combination of direct marketing, social media, paid advertising (print and online), and earned media (press coverage obtained through public relations efforts). Most events also feature a dedicated website that includes an online registration process and provides value-specific information to promote the event.

The old notion of B2B vs. B2C marketing (business-to-business vs. business-to-consumer) is obsolete. Every event participant is now a consumer because that's how they see themselves. Your event marketing plan should do more than sell registrations and floor space; it should enhance the perceived brand equity of your event, elevate your organization's larger brand efforts, and inspire committed participation.

Our four-phase methodology provides a useful way to think about all of these things, while creating an actionable plan for a successful, memorable event.

Glossary

Interviewing the subject matter experts (SMEs) who informed this book reminded us that industry professionals sometimes use one word to mean different things. For our purposes, we've assembled a list of frequently used terms, along with the meaning we usually imply when we use each of these terms.

Account lead—The person at the agency or general services contractor (GSC) who acts as a client's go-to team member. The account lead is responsible for conveying client needs and expectations to the event team, overseeing the efforts of other departments, understanding everything important about the client, and sharing new information. The account lead may collaborate with or double as the executive producer to manage the budget and may also lead the logistics team.

Agency—The marketing partner, production company, or GSC fulfilling event design and production on behalf of their client.

Audiovisual team (AV)—The team responsible for installing equipment used on the exhibition/trade show floor and for the "show" aspect of an event, including set design and production, lighting and audio design, crew staffing, and installing and dismantling the show itself. AV provides staging solutions and expertise and assists in the production of virtual, hybrid, and in-person events.

Association events—Events hosted by an association representing members who share a profession, industry, social or political cause, or other affiliation. Annual or semiannual conferences and trade shows bring their members together and provide opportunities for education and commerce. Association events typically charge fees to cover their costs and to raise funding for their overall mission, but their explicit purpose is serving members rather than generating profits or marketing their brand.

Content—Words, images, video, and other "contents" within a communication piece or publication. A content designer or a member of the creative team usually develops content.

Content designer—A member of the creative team who develops the messaging strategy for an event, including visual components and the text or scripts that accompany them. This person should be fluent in multiple forms of media and able to coordinate messaging across all platforms used during an event.

Core team—Members of all the key disciplines involved in the event from start to finish. This team usually includes an account lead, executive producer, creative director, and logistics expert, and may also include strategists, content designers, and experience designers.

Corporate events—One of the more useful channels in a corporation's marketing portfolio. Corporations may host their own specialized events or may sponsor or exhibit at events organized by others to maintain a brand presence at conferences and trade shows throughout the world. Unlike for-profit show organizers, events function as marketing tools for corporations, not as their core business.

Creative proposal—The response from the agency to an event creator's request for proposal (RFP). Strategic insights should inform creative proposals. The final draft of the creative proposal itself sometimes serves as the event plan.

Creative team—All the artists, designers, and writers responsible for the content, look, and feel of an event. A creative director typically leads the creative team, lending expertise from one or more of the critical disciplines.

Crisis-/risk-management plan—This is designed to address potential threats and hazards that could affect anyone on the show site: employees, customers, partners, and operations. This plan is intended to support and integrate with event-/venue-specific crisis-management plans and can also be tailored to show-specific safety/security procedures.

Design thinking—The perspective everyone working on an event should adopt to ensure that everything happens on purpose (by design) rather than by accident. This optimistic approach assumes improvement is always possible.

Designer—The professional who is responsible for the look, feel, sound, or shape of an event. Events require many types of designers, from exhibit designers to lighting designers.

Data and digital team—A group of professionals who deploy digital technology in strategic ways (one team or two distinct teams). This team develops a strategy to acquire and process the data used to refine the event design. This team may also help generate leads, register participants, and customize their experience, along with creating an interactive online experience to parallel, supplement, or replace the in-person event experience.

Event creator—The organization whose executives own final approval of the event plan and budget. As host of the event, the event creator determines who to invite to the event (the target audience); what kinds of sponsors, exhibitors, and media they hope to attract (if any); the essential purpose of the event; and when and where the event will take place. Event creators fall into three broad categories: corporate events driven by marketing strategy; for-profit show organizers and media companies with a full portfolio of events running throughout the year; and associations relying on the events they host to help fund their larger mission.

Event manager—The professional overseeing everything relating to the event, who reports to the executives hosting the event (the event creators). Sometimes referred to as *the show planner* or *show manager*, this person often collaborates with suppliers to coordinate all the moving parts and make sure everything runs according to plan. The event manager typically recommends locations, oversees arrangements handled by venue management, assigns exhibitor show floor space, arranges lodging and transportation for attendees, and contracts with caterers, guest presenters, entertainers, and other vendors.

Event plan—The document describing the purpose of the event, the essential metrics for success, the various elements included in the scope of the event, a timeline for developing the required deliverables, and a budget. This document could begin as an RFP from the event creator or as a response from the agency in the form of a creative proposal. The event plan represents an evolution of the strategy brief, opportunity document, creative brief, and/or creative proposal.

Event team—The professionals supporting the core team. Members of the event team represent various disciplines, attend team status meetings, and individually play a role in making the event happen.

Executive producer—The professional (sometimes also acting as account lead) responsible for supporting the event manager by executing the event plan and bringing it to life on time and within budget.

Exhibitor—A business paying a fee to showcase their product or service on the event floor. Exhibitor fees are based on location and square footage within the venue.

Exhibitor services—The group hired to meet the needs of exhibitors throughout the event (often a subgroup of the agency or GSC). In addition to helping exhibitors get the most value from their display, this group may establish and communicate regulations relating to the installation, maintenance, and dismantling of the exhibits; oversee materials handling, shipments, and deliveries; handle orders or rentals for exhibit creation; staff a dedicated call center to support exhibitors; and help exhibitors resolve any issues throughout the event. Exhibitor satisfaction reflects this team's responsiveness and effectiveness.

Experience designer—The professional who works with the creative/design team to visualize and design the entire event, focusing on how the five senses are engaged as attendees move through event properties. The experience designer creates renderings of decorations and activities, ensuring an attendee experience that meets the objectives described in the strategy brief/event plan.

Fabrication team—The professionals who create the event's scenic elements, exhibits, sets, signage, and props. Independent exhibitors may contract their own fabrication team or work with a GSC.

For-profit show organizer—An event-focused organization that maintains a full portfolio of dynamic market platforms that integrate live events and media to help promote learning and build businesses. This includes traditional media companies that host events as an extension of their brand, leveraging their database of subscribers to connect highly qualified buyers and sellers. Unlike corporate events that act as marketing channels to grow business, for-profit show organizers are in the business of producing events.

General services contractor (GSC)—A team of professionals (also known as *general contractors*) hired by the event creator to undertake and oversee physical set-up and tear-down of events (often in a convention center as part of a trade show). The GSC may be part of the agency or a separate entity. GSC duties may include inspecting the event site; preparing the floor layout; getting approvals from engineering and the venue's fire marshal; generating the online exhibitor kit; managing freight and storage for move-in and move-out; installing/removing all rigging; hiring and managing labor; and assigning space to each exhibitor.

Graphics—The visual aspects of banners, booths, exhibits, signage, and other design elements delivered by the design team, including everything from lanyards and badges to on-screen or projected images for presentations performed on a stage.

Logistics team—The team that coordinates the services offered by the GSC, manages the on-site implementation of the event plan, and handles loading a show into and out of a venue. The logistics team works with the event manager and exhibitors to deliver a wide range of services, from creating the exhibitor kit (establishing exhibit requirements and regulations) to the installation and dismantling of exhibits, hanging signage and banners, laying carpet, providing rented booth/stand furniture, contracting with union-represented workers, running wire and cables, securing and scheduling delivery trucks, and making sure everything is in place for the event and hauled away when it's over.

Marketing team—A group embedded in the event creator's organization or an independent agency, led by the chief marketing officer or their event manager. The marketing team focuses on ensuring the event strategically supports the brand and complements the larger marketing strategy. They may also manage event-specific communications, including registration and attendee messaging, websites, ads, press releases, and more.

Production team—One or more producers who make the event plan come to life. One producer may run the onstage general session events while other producers manage breakout sessions, gala parties, off-site excursions, or special events. This team reports to the executive producer and may be part of the larger agency or GSC team or may function as a separate company with its own contract.

RFP—A request for proposal. This document is created by a show organizer, association events team, corporate events team, or other event creator, declaring their intent to hire an agency or GSC to help produce the event. The RFP details essential information needed by the agency/ GSC for the submission of a creative proposal and budget.

Renaissance team—Shorthand for the diverse group of professionals assembled to formulate the best possible plan for an event. This group embodies the expertise, curiosity, imagination, demographic diversity, and worldview required to understand the challenges and opportunities represented by a proposed event.

Safety protocols—Protecting the health, safety, and welfare of the people building, staffing, and participating in the event is a top priority and must be managed. Safety concerns will vary depending on the venue and the nature of the planned events, but protocols must be established and enforced.

Show organizer—The event creator responsible for hosting an event, usually in the business of producing events to generate revenue. This term typically refers to for-profit companies that own, produce, or provide full-service management of in-person trade shows, consumer shows, expositions, conferences, and similar events as a core aspect of their business model.

Sponsor—An organization or brand that pays for their presence at an event, featuring exclusive privileges exceeding those of an exhibitor. These privileges might take the form of a title sponsorship, where the sponsor's logo is included on all communications and signage, or a sponsorship package giving the brand additional exposure with participants. Sponsors may add value by subsidizing the cost of some aspect of the event or by providing in-kind products or services.

Sponsorship team—A group charged with lining up sponsors who will pay for representation at the event, driving value for both the attendees and the sponsors. The sponsorship team may be part of the event manager's staff or a specialized agency team. They will typically create an array of enticing packages designed to strategically showcase sponsors to event participants and help offset event costs.

Strategy team—At least one strategist or group of strategists who work early in the event-planning phase to understand the purpose of the event and its key objectives. This team collects and analyzes all available information and provides the event-planning team with a vision of what's desirable, what's possible, and what challenges they'll face. The strategy team must understand the goals of the event creator's team, the needs of attendees and other stakeholders, and the definition of what *beautiful* looks like, so every member of the event team can help bring that vision to life. This process often results in a strategy brief that informs the event's creative and design efforts.

Sustainability team—May be a discrete team or designated champions within the larger event group who own accountability for managing the environmental impact of the event. This team often assumes responsibility for diversity, equity, and inclusion (DEI) as an important aspect of sustainability. This supports the shared belief that to achieve event goals, serve stakeholders, and deliver meaningful outcomes, teams must reflect the extraordinary range of human experience.

Venue—The location where the event will occur. A venue can be indoors, outdoors, or hosted at multiple locations. Often staged in convention centers, larger events may also utilize additional satellite locations. Conferences that don't include an exhibition area may take place in hotel ballrooms. Venues and host cities feature their own regulations and contracts regarding a wide range of items, from vendor requirements and union contracts to fire marshal regulations; the agency or GSC chosen to work with the event creator is often familiar with such requirements.

A WORD ABOUT WORDS

Having explained how we use the preceding terms in this book, we also feel obliged to offer a word of caution. Those of us working in the events industry sometimes forget to think like attendees. Regardless of an event's purpose or strategic priorities, its true goal should focus on bringing value to attendees. That means the words we use to engage them matter.

We suggest that it's time to alter our terminology when communicating with attendees. Instead of directing participants to the *general session* or *trade show exhibits*, we should invite them to the *inspirational session*, *solution discovery*, or *interactive learning*. Terms like *virtual* and *hybrid* are irrelevant to the attendee who already knows whether they will attend in person or remotely.

When we invite people into our circus tent, they come to see the trapeze artists, not the rigging. We hope that all event professionals can begin to use more attendee-centric terminology when communicating with attendees, and we urge everyone in the event community to adopt an attendee-friendly mindset.

GET STARTED

- Learn what's at stake

- Assemble and launch your team

- Define *beautiful* for this event

- Articulate the opportunity in a clear, concise statement

- Create a strategy document

- Choose your partners wisely

- Focus on budget, venue, and timeline

- Segment and define your target audience

- Build out your creative brief

- Implement a project-tracking system

Phase 1 is exciting, creative, and filled with possibility. In this initial phase, you'll start by building your team and asking yourselves these questions: What do we want to achieve? What will it look like when we get there? What resources will we require? Where are opportunities for taking things to the next level?

Then you'll engage with key stakeholders to define your shared vision, articulate a strategic direction, determine venue availability, understand your event design, and align your design with the event's strategic goals. You'll build an internal infrastructure for the project, including business intelligence, assets, goals, shared files, and anything else that will help get the job done. You'll also define your core team, a multidisciplinary group of people invested in the event's success and driven to pursue the event's goals.

This phase should conclude with an approved strategy document that, among other things, delineates your specific success metrics and drives your next steps.

CHAPTER 1

Build Your Team and Define *Beautiful*

TO-DO LIST:

- Understand what's at stake, and help your team understand what's at stake, at every turn.

- Remember that effective resource management is the backbone of any successful event.

- Surround yourself with committed professionals who push you to ask tough questions.

- Envision the best outcome for your event (the opportunity), and pursue that vision with every choice you make.

- Ensure effective efficiency by creating a collaborative environment where everyone contributes to the success of the event.

Working on an event begins by knowing everything you can about the event's goals. A keen, clear-eyed understanding of what's at stake with an event is crucial. You always want to know what's possible and what's at risk. Once you've assembled your team, you'll constantly ensure they know what's at risk, too, so they can be optimizing at every opportunity.

Your first steps will be ensuring that all involved parties reach consensus regarding the basic purpose, objectives, and goals of the planned event. You'll discuss the attendees, their expectations, and the ways attending your event will improve their lives. You'll delve into the specifics of planning and preparation, including an analysis of the resources at your disposal, budget, personnel, and materials, and you'll assess the availability and allocation of these resources to ensure they align with the event's objectives.

Effective resource management is the backbone of any successful event. It's not just about having enough resources but also about effective utilization of resources to minimize waste and maximize impact. You'll conduct thorough risk assessment and contingency planning; no event is immune to unforeseen challenges, whether logistic hiccups, weather-related difficulties, or last-minute changes in attendee numbers. Develop a comprehensive plan to address potential risks, ensuring that you have strategies in place to quickly resolve any issues that may arise. This proactive approach helps prepare you for the unexpected while instilling confidence in your team and stakeholders, demonstrating your commitment to the event's success.

Some essential action items to help you know what's at stake:

- **Review the background of this opportunity,** including existing debriefs. Address any of the previous event's shortcomings.

- **Describe the opportunity in detail,** delineating what's possible and what the keys to success will be.

- **Note the top three objectives for the event** in order of priority, and list the benefits they will yield.

- **Familiarize yourself with accurate details about available funds,** and determine whether the budget is fixed or dependent on factors such as sponsorship support.

- **Create a rough timeline for the project,** working backward from the target delivery date.

Ensure that every element of the event you're planning aligns with the predefined, agreed-upon, overarching purpose. An event's success isn't measured solely by smooth execution, but also by the impact it makes on its guests.

With meticulous preparation, thoughtful resource allocation, and an eye always on your objectives, you're now ready to start turning this vision into a memorable reality by building your team, briefing your team, and ensuring they're ready to execute the plan.

An event's success isn't measured solely by smooth execution, but also by the impact it makes on its guests.

BUILD YOUR RENAISSANCE TEAM

Diversity, equity, and inclusion (DEI) policies continue to be a priority with most large organizations. It's good business sense to have a diverse range of team members who reflect the different perspectives of the event's target customers. Further, it is essential to effective collaboration that the various teams accountable for fulfilling the plan have a voice in its creation.

For our purposes, a Renaissance team refers to the group of people you'll assemble to formulate the best possible plan for the desired event. Combined, these individuals embody the expertise, curiosity, imagination, demographic diversity, and worldview to understand the challenges and opportunities represented by the proposed event. Those chosen should have the discipline and grace to collaborate on a variety of viable solutions and recommendations without turning brainstorming sessions into a competition. Surround yourself with a quorum of people who push you to ask tough questions.

STEPS IN BUILDING YOUR RENAISSANCE TEAM

- Work to include professionals who reflect the values, interests, and perspectives of your audience and stakeholders. Diversity is always essential but is especially so early in the planning process. Many of those professionals who bring a uniquely informed perspective to the brainstorming process, such as subject matter experts (SMEs), may not need to continue contributing after initial plans are approved.

- Assemble a diverse event team that includes members from every key department, discipline, or operation necessary for the event. Involve every member of this team as early in the project as possible. Event development will dictate when each team member becomes engaged in the project, based on their responsibilities. Proactively prepare all required onboarding steps to bring each new team member up to speed quickly when they join the team.

- Identify the lead for each discipline—your core team—and define their roles and responsibilities. For example, an account lead, strategic lead, production lead, and creative/design lead.

- Kick off the project by sharing all background information and initial thoughts on the project with the team. Plan and maintain regular project updates and check-ins with key team members.

Not everyone on this initial "kickoff" Renaissance team will stay on as a permanent part of the event team; some of these professionals will act only in an advisory capacity or as SMEs. In that case, let them know up front exactly what will be expected of them. For example, if you're planning an event that targets musicians, you may invite an acquaintance who performs in the local symphony to help answer questions and vet the team's initial thinking. Once they've shared their expertise and helped inform or validate your strategic plan, you can cut them loose.

Defining essential roles and choosing the right people to be part of your event team from day one will ensure that all critical functional areas are represented and that those teams know what's coming their way. This practice also effectively launches your event-planning activities with good project management. You can help ensure the success of your event through meticulous planning and team coordination.

PRO TIPS:

- Empathy is a design mandate. It's your responsibility to listen carefully to your stakeholders; it's also your job to tell them what they need to hear based on your expertise, experience, and professional commitment.

- Sales growth may be an event's ultimate goal, but that's not a sustainable plan if no one is interested in attending the event.

- The heart of strategic event planning is listening to what stakeholders say they want, looking at what they actually do, and then articulating the value proposition that will take them there. One of your primary goals is to make stakeholders glad they participated in your event and motivated to fulfill your objectives.

BUILDING YOUR RENAISSANCE TEAM

1. Recruitment and selection process:

- **Identify core competencies:** Before you begin your recruiting efforts, list the core competencies and skills needed for each role on your team. This clarity will help you in the selection process to ensure candidates fit the role while complementing team dynamics.

- **Seek out diverse skill sets:** Look for candidates with a range of experiences and backgrounds. Diversity in skills and perspectives can foster creativity and innovation, leading to a more successful event.

- **Leverage various recruitment channels:** Access a mix of channels to attract a wide range of candidates, from industry-specific job boards and social media platforms to professional networking events and internal company talent pools.

- **Conduct structured interviews:** Implement a structured interview process that assesses technical skills and cultural fit. Include scenario-based questions that can help provide useful insights into how candidates handle typical or atypical event-planning challenges, and their ability to work under pressure, solve problems, and collaborate with a team. Consider involving key team members in the selection process to help assess how new hires will interact with existing team dynamics.

2. Early engagement and information sharing:

- **Kickoff meeting:** Once your team is in place, conduct a comprehensive kickoff meeting in which you focus on setting expectations, outlining the event's vision, and ensuring that everyone is adequately informed and correctly aligned with their roles and responsibilities. Use this opportunity to inspire your team and help everyone understand the big picture and see how their contributions fit into it. Use visual aids, interactive tools, or storytelling techniques to make the vision and strategy as compelling and clear as possible.

- **Pre-meeting preparation:** Before every meeting (including these first ones) distribute an agenda and materials outlining the event's vision and objectives. You want your team members to come to meetings prepared to engage and contribute meaningfully.

- **Breakout sessions:** Following main presentations, organize breakout sessions where small groups can discuss how they can contribute to achieving the vision, enabling tailored discussions and creative brainstorming.

- **Rotating leadership:** Have different team members lead meetings to foster a sense of ownership and bring fresh perspectives to how meetings are conducted.

- **Detailed project plan:** Develop a detailed project plan dedicated specifically to each team member that includes their own timelines, milestones, and deliverables. Use project management tools to keep everyone updated on progress and changes.

- **Regular check-ins and updates:** Establish a routine of regular meetings in which updates help team members stay aware of what's coming their way so they can prepare accordingly. These meetings also provide a forum for addressing any issues or roadblocks early on.

- **Encourage open communication, teamwork, and problem-solving** among team members and through regular team meetings, a dedicated communication channel, or an open-door policy with project leaders.

- A **collaborative culture** empowers your team to share ideas, provide support, and work together efficiently toward the event's success.

continued

- Ensure that feedback leads to **actionable steps** when appropriate, from adjusting plans to addressing concerns or implementing suggested improvements, demonstrating a responsive, adaptive management approach.

- **Leverage technology for real-time communication:** Choose communication tools that best fit your team's size, needs, and preferences.

  - Tech companies are always updating and improving product offerings designed to support business groups that rely on secure instant messaging, task management, and video calls, which encourage interaction and content sharing; the right technology helps streamline communication.

  - Integrate your communication tools with project management software to allow seamless updates and notifications across platforms, keeping everyone informed and engaged in real time.

- Provide **training** and support for any technology or software being used to help prevent technical difficulties from hindering communication.

3. Launching with solid project management:

- **Project management tools:** Employ project management software to track tasks, deadlines, and dependencies. Tools like those offered by Microsoft and Google can help keep everyone on track and facilitate communication across teams.

- **Risk management planning:** Identify potential risks at the outset and develop mitigation strategies. This proactive approach helps everyone manage unforeseen challenges without derailing the event-planning process.

- **Resource management:** Carefully plan your resources and budget as early as you can to help ensure that you can deliver the event without compromising on quality or scope. Make sure you and your team prioritize managing vendor contracts, sponsorship funds, and team resources effectively right from the start.

- **Continuous learning and adaptation:** Encourage a culture of ongoing education, growth, sharing, and responsiveness within your team.

  - At every step, starting early on, discuss what's working well and what can be improved.

  - This feedback loop will refine your event-planning processes and enhance team performance over time.

  - Be prepared to adjust your plans and strategies based on feedback and the realities of your project's progress.

  - Making these adjustments helps your team stay agile and respond to unexpected challenges.

By focusing on these strategic aspects of team building and project management, you're taking powerful steps to help ensure that your event-planning process starts off with effective efficiency. You're creating a collaborative environment where everyone is prepared, informed, and motivated to contribute to the success of the event. You're also building a solid foundation for future successes.

Members of the core team should consult to decide who will participate in the Renaissance team's initial kickoff session. A representative from each discipline required to produce the event should attend, including audiovisual, creative services, design/graphics, digital, exhibitor services, fabrication, logistics, production services, sponsorship, talent acquisition, logistics, and any other special expertise indicated by your strategic insights. Include vintage auto enthusiasts when planning a vintage car show; invite active gamers when planning a video gaming conference. Initial brainstorming may reveal additional areas of expertise to seek out.

If you are the account lead or strategist leading the first session, your tactical assignment may be briefing Renaissance team members on the opportunities and challenges involved in the assignment, but your primary goal is to inspire them. Do you want them to focus just on filling floor space or to actively enable the innovative problem-solving that could kindle amazing positive change in the world? It's all about how you frame the opportunity and what *beautiful* looks like to you.

WHAT DOES *BEAUTIFUL* LOOK LIKE?

What does *beautiful* look like in the context of this unique live event? Visualizing your ideal outcomes—what you hope to see after the event concludes—is a useful method for illuminating an event's challenges and opportunities.

Ask the team to describe the most beautiful outcome they can imagine. Everyone on the event team should work to understand what *beautiful* looks like and implement a plan to get there. Perhaps beautiful looks like a powerful confluence of audience engagement, seamless logistics, stunning visuals, and an unforgettable experience that lingers in the minds of attendees long after they leave the event.

1. Identify your event's unique aesthetic.

- Every event features its own distinct character and vibe. Decide what makes your event stand out. Is it the elegance of a gala, the energy of a concert, or the innovation of a tech conference?

- Involve the team in the vision. Encourage each team member to contribute their ideas of what a beautiful outcome would look like for this event. The collective vision resulting from this collaborative brainstorm will help create a cohesive, impactful event.

2. Set the stage for the event's brand of visual beauty.

- Visualize the event space by using 3D modeling and virtual walk-throughs to envisage the event setup. How will the lighting play with the architecture? Where will the focal points be?

- Prioritize the sensory experience by thinking beyond visuals and considering how the event will appeal to all senses. The right mix of sound, lighting, and scent can elevate every aspect of the experience.

3. Logistic elegance makes beauty happen.

- Seamless flow ensures that every logistic aspect, from entry to exit, is smooth and hassle-free, from crowd management to transportation and accessibility.

- Crisis management prepares you for the unexpected. A beautiful event is one where challenges are managed gracefully and efficiently.

4. Audience engagement makes the beauty real.

- Know your audience and tailor the experience to their expectations and preferences. What would make the event beautiful, meaningful, and memorable for them?

- Incorporate elements that engage the audience actively, from interactive installations to social media integration or live polling.

5. Sustainable beauty empowers a responsible approach.

- Eco-friendly practices incorporate sustainability in your event planning. Use recyclable materials, minimize waste, and opt for digital solutions over paper when it makes sense.

- Printed materials that are designed with beauty and the intent to serve as a keepsake or collectible piece may be

continued

valued by eco-friendly audiences; make sure your giveaways are worth keeping and not destined for the landfill.

- Community involvement engages local vendors and communities in your event. This collaboration supports local economies while adding unique local flavor to the event.

6. Reflection and feedback improve beauty. What did you learn from the previous event? What will you want to have learned when this one concludes?

- Review available, relevant debrief documents from previous events.

- Plan now to conduct a thorough post-event analysis and debriefing session; what needs to be in place to document the opportunities and challenges encountered while making your dream of beauty come to life?

- Gather feedback from past attendees and stakeholders. This insight is invaluable for refining the concept of beauty going forward.

Creating a beautiful outcome for your event requires balancing vision, execution, and adaptability. By deciding and understanding what *beauty* means for your event and strategically planning to achieve this vision, you can transform your live event into an extraordinary experience. Beauty isn't just seen—it's felt, lived, and remembered.

Now that you've defined your goals, built your team, and agreed on your shared vision, it's time to get down to brass tacks. Get ready to build your strategy document, the blueprint for your live event's construction.

PRO TIPS:

- If your goals call for significantly improved or different results, doing things the same way will never work. Establishing a diverse team of thinkers (Renaissance team) early on in the planning process provokes fresh thinking.

- A data-based strategic plan that systematically considers what beautiful looks like—that is, how you'll know you've been successful— should inform each step that will take you there. Work backward from where you want to arrive to think about the required steps.

Build Your Strategy Document

TO-DO LIST:

- Create a purposeful strategy document designed to fulfill the opportunity and meet the event's goals.

- Remember that the event's vision and mission (offering guidance and direction) aren't its goals (measurable achievements).

- As you work, always ask questions and look for what's new in the world surrounding the event.

The outcome of all your preliminary research, team building, and brainstorming should be the creation of your strategy document, which will prioritize the top objectives for the event, frame up the work that needs to be done, and help familiarize everyone on the team with their primary focus going forward.

HOW TO CREATE A STRATEGY DOCUMENT

Throughout the first phase, it's essential for you to capture all the key concepts and strategies that will inform the design phase within your strategy document (a strategic assessment or creative brief). This document may be initiated in response to an RFP from the event manager or to an opportunity brief created by an account lead at the agency or GSC. The strategist formulates the strategy document; the creative director utilizes it to inspire brainstorming sessions and direct progress. The document's job is to ensure alignment between the key parties (those executing the event and those in approval positions). Make sure that anyone authorized to modify, approve, or kill your plan signs off on this document before you proceed to the next phase.

A SUCCESSFUL STRATEGY DOCUMENT'S VITAL COMPONENTS

Crafting a strategy document is like plotting a boat's course across a vast ocean: It acts as a navigational chart that directs a team toward their destination. Before setting goals, define the event's vision and mission, as these principles provide guidance and direction but distinguish them from its goals, which represent measurable achievements.

> **Crafting a strategy document is like plotting a boat's course across a vast ocean: It acts as a navigational chart that directs a team toward their destination.**

1. Establish clear objectives
2. Embrace decisiveness
3. Craft a clear, compelling structure

These three critical elements of an effective strategy document will help keep things on track:

1. Establish clear objectives

While it might seem obvious, many strategy documents fail to articulate concrete objectives. Instead of setting tangible goals, they default to vague aspirations ("achieve growth") without setting specific goals, making it more difficult to develop effective strategies and allocate resources efficiently.

Formulate objectives that are precise, attainable, and in harmony with your strategic vision for the event. Create SMART goals aligned with your event's overall strategy.

- **S**pecific: Define clear objectives for the event.

- **M**easurable: Establish metrics to track progress and key performance indicators (KPIs), facilitating monitoring.

- **A**chievable: Avoid overly ambitious goals; instead, focus on realistic targets for your event.

- **R**elevant: Ensure each goal's alignment with the vision and mission for the event.

- **T**ime-bound: Schedule deadlines for each goal to create urgency and accountability.

2. Embrace decisiveness

- Tough choices are always part of strategy creation, and often one of its most challenging aspects. Many event organizers struggle to prioritize, deny the feasibility of long-term strategy decisions, or focus on the easier decisions involved in optimizing the status quo.

- A strategy document decisively answers fundamental questions, including defining your scope (industry, geography, customer segments, etc.) and identifying your unique competitive advantage. Equally crucial is deciding

continued

and specifying what you will not pursue (even though this information might not appear explicitly in the final document).

- While it might seem tempting to keep your strategy broad and open to unforeseen opportunities, an indecisive approach that lacks focus hinders your event's potential for success. Your scope and competitive advantage should be crystal clear; if you can't succinctly articulate them on a single page, revisit the exercise.

- Some strategy documents list well-intentioned initiatives, with teams attempting to reverse engineer goals from tactics (an ill-advised approach). If an initiative in the strategy document can't be directly tied to the event's objectives and overarching goals, it should be omitted and resources redirected. Even the best ideas must align with the chosen strategy if they're to be implemented.

3. Craft a clear, compelling structure

Your strategy document should be logically organized, easy to understand, visually appealing, and should read like an engaging, straightforward narrative.

- **Define** your event's destination (vision/mission + SMART goals).

- **Identify** your event's major focus areas and initiatives.

- **Divide** everything into executable tasks (sub-initiatives, tactics, specific actions toward goals).

- **Translate** this plan into a practical timeline, including details on resource allocation.

The actionable road map you end up with will outline goals, initiatives, timelines, responsibilities, budgets, and resource allocation. Periodically review and update your strategy doc's road map to adapt to changes. By following these guidelines, you can create a strategy document that helps your event achieve its goals while adapting to an ever-changing landscape.

Get full buy-in from everyone authorized to modify, approve, or kill your plan before you proceed.

WHILE YOU'RE BUILDING THE STRATEGY DOCUMENT:
Ask the Right Questions

Assign someone qualified to explore, list, understand, and explain the full scope of the event's foreseeable challenges and opportunities and formulate a strategy. This person will usually be the strategist, but they can't operate in a vacuum; in some organizations, the core team works together through these steps to jointly develop the strategy.

Strategists who work for an agency (not for the event creator) tend to start this process by collecting everything they can find out about the client's business and branding. If the agency's account lead maintains a client dossier, that information can be very helpful. After the strategist obtains all available information, they dig deeper into the opportunity and challenge existing assumptions. For example, they will ask executives who work with the event manager: Do you really want to hold this event or create this exhibit space? Why is this the best use of your marketing dollars? Where does this event fit in with your larger marketing plan and with the priorities of your entire enterprise? What should participants do as they leave the event? How do you hope to change their behavior? How will you demonstrate the value of the event experience so that participants sing your praises and plan to return to your next event? What about this event will attract exhibitors, partners, and sponsors (if that is a goal)?

The team then consolidates all relevant information gained from this line of questioning into the strategy document, which will evolve as the strategy itself changes and expands. Someone (ideally the strategist) must take ownership to ensure that strategy documentation continues in a linear path, so critical insights aren't lost when the path shifts or when a new team takes the lead.

Identify Challenges and Opportunities

If this is an annual or recurring event, the strategist will seek out answers in the debrief notes from the previous event (hopefully someone captured them). This information will help the planner identify the big wins and painful lessons from the previous event. The strategist will review this information to evaluate what worked and what didn't and flag opportunities for improvement or new ideas for engagement. It's advisable to get an early start documenting the decisions and outcomes shaping the current event to inform phase 4's "review and improve" sessions and assist in planning next year's event.

The strategist should interview stakeholders to understand their perspective and evaluate the event creator's available research or conduct a quick survey. The strategist may begin by conducting a simple SWOT (strengths, weaknesses, opportunities, and threats) analysis with a representative group of stakeholders, an effective method for obtaining a snapshot of what's at stake. The strategist should also bring fresh research to the table, from new information about current market trends to breakthroughs within the business sector or developments within the event world.

Track What's New

Seek out and review any information that might reveal new insights by organizing and conducting interviews, surveys, or focus groups to understand the priorities of the key stakeholders and how they may have shifted. The list of stakeholders usually includes the event creator team; their primary audience, which could include association members, employees, franchisees, or paying members of the public; event sponsors; event exhibitors; and the community representing the host city or venue. Assuming the event occurs annually, the strategist can start by investigating previous years' events and assessing evolution, growth, and change.

Listen carefully to what stakeholders think while tactically pushing back to avoid repeating ineffective approaches or elements, ensuring relevance and bringing value to all the stakeholders. Always looking for "what's new" in the world surrounding the event is key to avoiding obsolescence. The strategist aims to understand what's changed, including any recently emerging factors that could affect the context of the event or the engagement of its attendees.

Examine news reports, white papers, influencer social media posts, and related sources that might point to shifts in trends or interests, whether driven by new technology, sociopolitical concerns, demographic shifts, or any input that signals change. The local tourism board, chamber of commerce, or convention and visitor bureau can act as a useful resource during early opportunity exploration. Working with a destination management company (DMC) that specializes in knowing what the host city offers can uncover unique opportunities for attendees to immerse themselves in local attractions.

The importance of this search for what's new especially pertains to events that are held annually or more frequently. Events often fall into a rut, doing the same thing every year. Never assume that what's always worked will continue working in a world that's constantly changing.

AUTHENTIC NETWORKING

Events are increasingly encouraging decentralized, casual networking opportunities that feel organic to the experience. Leverage authentic opportunities for interaction at your event in a number of ways.

- **Encourage crowdsourced content,** from sessions to meetups to mentoring sessions. Some major conferences allocate dedicated space that attendee groups can sign up for and use on-site. For example, SXSW film festival offers open voting for proposed sessions at each upcoming gathering.

continued

- **Leverage the power of peer-to-peer.** Encourage topic-driven conversations—at dedicated lunch tables, in meetup zones, or through casual opportunities to participate in wellness activities, running groups, or golf.

- **Watch people and learn.** Take time (or hire someone) to conduct an ethnographic study of your event. Analyze where people congregate, how they interact, and when they formalize their plans. New audience-tracking technologies can monitor volume, dwell time, and even sentiment, then deliver meaningful insights.

- **Partner with connectors, linchpins, and influencers.** Seek out people who are good at making connections and who understand your audience(s) better than anyone. Hire them to engage with your audience and drive attendance.

- **Join social media groups.** Focus on knowledge-sharing or community-building groups geared toward specific like-minded topics.

For every opportunity you provide attendees to network, try to deliver at least three tangible benefits. Next, it's critical to anchor the opportunity in terms of these three essentials: location, funding, and time. Each of these conditions informs the others.

PRO TIPS:

- **To declutter your strategy document,** create two lists: what will change and what won't change.

- **To further strategize your strategy document,** list the obstacles you'll need to overcome, detail methods for overcoming those obstacles, and create a scoreboard to measure your team's progress.

- **Ask stakeholders this question:** *If you had to cut out something you've always done at previous events, what would it be?* Event planners often include costly features simply because they think it's required.

CHAPTER 3

Think in Threes

TO-DO LIST:

- Make your own "Top Threes" list to help prioritize.

- Choose your collaborators wisely.

- Remember that venue, budget, and time are three of the most important elements of your event.

LIST YOUR TOP THREES

Many teams benefit from fleshing out a "Top Threes" list to keep the entire team focused. Creating a simple one-page document proves useful for new team members who need to be quickly brought up to speed and for managing new ideas or unexpected changes in direction. Summarizing key project considerations in an easy-to-reference format, the Top Threes list facilitates planning, helps all related disciplines evaluate their performance, aligns various stakeholders, and provides a lens for rating the relative merit of various proposed solutions.

You can customize a Top Threes format to make whatever works best for your needs, but here are some ways to start producing and organizing your Top Threes.

- Start by listing your top three event objectives (as validated by the event manager and other team members).
- For each objective, list three ways it will be tracked and measured (i.e., KPIs).
- List the three primary audience groups.
- Include three short, insightful statements about the opportunity.
- Add three more with crucial information (challenges, limitations, etc.).
- If branding is a vital aspect of the event, list three aspects of the brand promise that must be reflected in the brand.
- If you are an agency bidding on an assignment, write three statements that capture your unique advantage to include in any pitches or presentations.

Continue with more Top Threes until you feel you have everything you need.

Top Three Venue Considerations

1. **Accessibility:** List three ways the venue is accessible to all participants, including those with disabilities.

2. **Capacity and layout:** Identify three key features of the venue's capacity and layout that make it ideal for your event's specific needs (e.g., breakout rooms, main stage, exhibition space).

3. **Technology and infrastructure:** Ensure the venue has three essential technology and infrastructure capabilities (e.g., Wi-Fi, AV equipment, on-site technical support).

Top Three Vendor Management Strategies

1. **Selection criteria:** Define three main criteria for selecting vendors (price, quality, reliability).

2. **Communication plan:** Outline three key components of your communication plan with vendors to ensure clarity and efficiency.

3. **Contingency plans:** Have three contingency plans in place for critical vendors (e.g., catering, AV, security) in case of last-minute cancellations or failures.

Top Three Marketing and Promotion Tactics

1. **Target audience channels:** Identify the three most effective channels for reaching your event's target audience (e.g., social media platforms, email marketing, industry publications).

2. **Messaging strategy:** Craft three core messages that resonate with your target audience and underline the value of attending your event.

3. **Engagement metrics:** Choose three key metrics to measure the success of your marketing efforts (e.g., registration numbers, social media engagement, website traffic).

Top Three Participant Engagement Strategies

1. **Interactive sessions:** Plan for three types of interactive sessions to boost engagement (e.g., workshops, Q&A sessions, panel discussions).

2. **Networking opportunities:** Facilitate three distinct networking opportunities for attendees (e.g., speed networking, dedicated networking zones, networking apps).

3. **Feedback mechanisms:** Implement three ways to collect feedback from participants (e.g., live polls, feedback forms, social media engagement).

Top Three Risk Management Steps

1. **Risk assessment:** Conduct a thorough risk assessment and identify the three major potential risks for your event (e.g., weather, security, health and safety).

2. **Mitigation strategies:** Develop mitigation strategies for each identified risk to minimize impact.

3. **Emergency response plan:** Establish a comprehensive emergency response plan that includes three key components (evacuation procedures, medical emergency response, communication plan).

Top Three Sustainability Practices

1. **Waste reduction:** Implement three initiatives to reduce waste at your event (e.g., digital programs, reusable materials, food donation programs).

2. **Energy efficiency:** Choose a venue that meets three criteria for energy efficiency (e.g., LED lighting, energy-efficient HVAC systems, green building certification).

3. **Sustainable transportation:** Encourage three sustainable transportation options for attendees (e.g., public transportation, bike sharing, carpooling incentives).

By incorporating these "Top Threes" into your event-planning process, you can create a well-rounded and effective strategy that covers various aspects of event management, from logistics and vendor relations to marketing, engagement, and sustainability. This structured approach helps ensure that every element of the event is considered and managed efficiently, leading to a successful and memorable experience for all involved.

Once the core team agrees on these Top Threes, the account lead or strategist can consult with other team members to finalize the success metrics and ensure that required data points are captured in the course of event production. Identify three ways to track and measure each of the three objectives, then clarify which team members own execution, analysis, and reporting. For some events, this process could be as simple as surveys taken before and after the event. Others will require a complex interaction of data-capture points, perhaps from proximity-sensing apps on participants' devices, physical beacons on the show floor tracking traffic, or other digital engagements that indicate participant satisfaction.

ADVICE TO THE EVENT MANAGER ON CHOOSING PARTNERS

The quality and support of your partners can make or break your event. Experience design, digital content, logistics, hospitality, production—the list of specialized services will be as long as the unique requirements of your event. Often, many of these services will be provided by a single partner, making things easier to manage. Or you may have long-standing relationships with diverse partners who collaborate well with others.

When choosing your partners, first confirm capabilities, experience, and creative problem-solving through testing and quality assurance processes. Find out how they handle unexpected changes and disruptions. Determine whether you can trust them to push back if they decide you're making bad choices or overlooking some of your options. Surround yourself with people who push you to ask tough questions. Breathe new life into a tired event by trusting the right partners to bring you news on the latest trends, insights gleaned from other industries, and fresh thinking to take your event to the next level.

Want more ways to use threes? Choose your top three partners for any task and then do something that helps maintain good relationships with them. List your top three expectations for each task you assign. Detail your top three requirements for any service you retain.

Creating a successful live event requires meticulous planning and execution but also hinges on the strength and quality of your partnerships. Choosing the right partners is crucial and can dramatically influence the outcome of your event. Select your partners with responsibility and due diligence.

- **Assess comprehensive capabilities:** Before engaging with a partner, thoroughly assess their ability to meet the wide-ranging needs of your event. This assessment should cover their expertise in areas critical to your event's success. Determine whether a potential partner can offer a multifaceted service package or if you'll need to engage multiple entities.

- **Verify experience and track record:** A potential partner's experience and past performance are paramount. Look for partners with a proven track record in handling events similar to yours. You may need to examine case studies, request references, or review portfolios of past events they've supported. A partner's ability to showcase their involvement in successful events is a testament to their capability and reliability.

- **Evaluate creative problem-solving skills:** Events often face unforeseen challenges, so it's ideal to have a partner who can think on their feet, offer creative solutions, and scale up or down as needed. During your selection process, discuss potential scenarios or past instances where they've had to navigate difficulties. You're looking for insight into their problem-solving prowess and adaptability.

- **Test for quality assurance:** Implement testing and quality assurance processes to confirm that your potential partner can deliver on their promises. You might require trial runs, pilot projects, or detailed discussions on their quality control measures. Ensuring they uphold stringent standards for quality and performance will help mitigate risks and elevate the overall event experience.

- **Question handling of unexpected changes:** Query prospective partners on their protocols for managing unexpected changes or disruptions. Ask them about sudden venue changes, technology failures, or last-minute adjustments in event scheduling. A partner's preparedness and flexibility in handling such situations may be critical for maintaining the smooth flow of your event.

- **Check for constructive feedback and pushback:** Select partners who are willing to provide honest feedback and pushback on decisions that may not be in the best interest of the event. This trait is essential for fostering a collaborative environment where all parties are committed to achieving the best possible outcome. A partner's willingness to challenge ideas constructively can be instrumental in avoiding potential pitfalls.

- **Seek fresh perspectives and innovation:** In today's fast-evolving event landscape, staying abreast of the latest trends and innovations is crucial. Opt for partners who are known for their forward-thinking approach and research-driven creative. Their ability to bring fresh insights and ideas can add spark to your event and help ensure it stands out.

- **Prioritize effective collaboration:** Given the complex nature of events, it's essential for your partners to be able to work collaboratively with other stakeholders. Look for entities that have a history of successful collaborations and can seamlessly integrate with other teams and partners. This synergy can be a huge contributor to a smooth, cohesive event.

- **Confirm financial stability and reliability:** Confirm the financial health of your partners, ensuring that they have the stability and resources to see the project through

continued

to completion. Prevent unexpected complications by conducting some level of due diligence or by requesting financial assurances to mitigate any risks.

· **Evaluate communication and transparency:** Effective communication and transparency throughout the planning and execution phases are vital. Partners should be forthcoming with information, responsive to inquiries, and proactive in updating you on progress and potential issues. Establishing clear communication channels and expectations from the outset is key to a successful partnership.

· **Consider post-event support and analysis:** Invite partners to contribute after the event. Partners that provide post-event analysis and feedback can offer insights that improve future events.

Creating a successful live event that leaves a lasting impression on attendees hinges not just on the internal team's effort but significantly on the choice of external partners. Choosing the right partners for your event requires careful consideration of their capabilities, experience, adaptability, and alignment with your event's goals—and is a critical decision. Form partnerships that meet and exceed the expectations for your event, ensuring its success and the satisfaction of all stakeholders involved.

VENUE, TIMELINE, AND BUDGET: THREE VITAL ITEMS

Venue

1. Start planning early

   Advance booking: Most events are planned well in advance—often years—allowing for the venue to be secured and all details to be meticulously arranged. This early start is crucial for locking in dates and ensuring the venue fits the event's specific needs. The event manager may secure a venue before engaging with agencies, so it's important to understand the opportunities and limitations this imposes on the event plan.

2. Consult experts before finalizing the venue

    Special requirements consideration: Before signing any contracts, it's essential to consult with experts, especially if the event has unique needs (e.g., showcasing large equipment, hosting live animals, organizing drone flyovers, etc.), as some venues are better equipped for, or more welcoming of, specialized requirements. Some big ideas are only possible in highly specialized locations. Carefully investigate venue selection choices before committing.

3. Select a venue that supports your vision

    Bringing your team's vision for the event to life: Understand that not all venues can accommodate every concept. If your event design involves unconventional structures, attractions, or setups, selecting a venue that can support your event's unique demands is key to realizing your vision.

4. Think of your venue as a campus

    Staging unique experiences: A venue should be more than just a place; it should be a campus covered with a range of unique experiences, enhancing the value of attending and allowing participants to engage deeply with the event and its elements.

5. Leverage off-campus excursions

    Creating added value and sponsorship opportunities: Incorporating off-campus excursions can significantly enhance the attendee experience and open up new sponsorship opportunities by encouraging guests to explore the host city and engage in unique, memorable local or campus-adjacent experiences.

6. Work with a destination management company (DMC)

    Discovering unique opportunities: Partnering with a DMC can provide valuable local insights and access to unique opportunities that might not be apparent from the outset. A DMC can help tailor experiences that immerse attendees in the host city's culture and attractions, adding another layer of engagement to your event.

7. Engage with the host city's tourism board

    Extended-stay packages: Consulting the host city's tourism board can uncover opportunities to create extended-stay packages for your guests. These packages can encourage attendees to explore the city further, turning the event into a more enriching experience and potentially boosting local tourism.

8. Consider the overall attendee experience

    Beyond the event itself: When planning your event, think deeper than just the immediate schedule to consider the overall attendee experience. From the moment they arrive to the time they leave, every aspect of their journey should be considered and enhanced wherever possible.

9. Innovate and adapt

    Stay open to new ideas: The world of event planning is always evolving, with new technologies and trends emerging regularly. Stay open to innovation and consider how you can incorporate new ideas into your venue selection to stay ahead of the curve.

10. Sustainability matters

    Eco-friendly choices: Attendees value sustainability. Selecting a venue that prioritizes eco-friendly practices and planning your event with sustainability in mind reduces environmental impact while enhancing the event's appeal to environmentally conscious audiences.

Timeline

Creating a detailed, accurate, effective timeline is pivotal for the success of any event. This timeline guides event-planning managers and their teams through each phase of the process, from initial concept to post-event analysis. Here's how to build a timeline that helps ensure an event that unfolds successfully.

1. Establish your event's foundation

    The journey to plan and execute the event begins in earnest the moment the venue has been secured, because the big questions "when and where" have been answered. This critical first step locks in the event dates and anchors your entire planning process, providing a fixed target your whole team must meet. Here is where you start to plot out your timeline, detailing every item up to the day of the event.

2. Work backward to create a rough timeline

    Reverse engineer your success: Starting with the event date, map out each step in reverse. Among other benefits, this approach helps you allocate enough time for each task and ensures you don't overlook critical deadlines.

    Engage with your team: Collaboration is key. Bring your team together to draft this preliminary timeline. Each member's input can help identify essential tasks and realistic time frames, ensuring your timeline is comprehensive and achievable.

3. Highlight key milestones and tasks

    Identify major milestones: Break down the event into major milestones such as venue booking, vendor contracts, ticket sales launch, and marketing campaigns. Assigning specific deadlines to these milestones will help keep your planning on track.

    Detail the tasks required: For each milestone, list the tasks that need to be completed. This breakdown transforms your timeline from a high-level overview into a detailed action plan, guiding your team through the execution phase.

4. Identify and address pinch points

    Spot potential budget and schedule risks early: As you flesh out your timeline, keep an eye out for pinch points—moments where delays, cost overruns, or resource shortages could derail your event. Identifying these risks early allows you to work on mitigating them before they become critical issues.

    Plan for contingencies: For each identified pinch point, develop contingency plans. Whether it's a backup vendor list, additional budget allocation, or alternative scheduling options, being prepared for the unexpected is crucial.

5. Plan for ongoing timeline management

    Regularly review and update sessions: Your event timeline is not set in stone. Regularly revisiting and updating it with your team ensures that you can adapt to changes and address any delays or challenges as they arise.

Effectively communicate: Ensure that updates to the timeline are communicated promptly to all stakeholders. Keeping everyone informed prevents confusion and ensures that the team remains cohesive and focused on common goals.

Implementing the Timeline: Three Tools

To bring this strategy to life, consider these three tools:

Project management software: Utilize digital tools designed for project management. Your team probably already has a favorite, and these are being updated and expanded all the time. Make sure the platform you use includes features that can help you create, track, and update your timeline with ease. The most popular tools also facilitate team collaboration, making it easier to assign tasks, set deadlines, and monitor progress.

Check-ins and adjustments: Schedule regular check-in meetings with your team to review the timeline's progress. These meetings are crucial for addressing any roadblocks and making necessary adjustments to keep the event planning on track.

Visualization: Consider using Gantt charts, infographics, or other visual aids to represent your timeline. A visual representation can help you and your team quickly grasp the sequence of tasks, durations, and overlaps, making it easier to manage the overall project.

Meticulously creating and managing a focused timeline helps teams navigate the complexities of event organization smoothly. A reverse-engineered timeline approach helps ensure that all critical tasks are completed in a timely manner and enhances the team's ability to deliver an exceptional event experience.

Budget

Mastering the art of budget management can help guarantee the success of any event. Here's how to navigate budget parameters skillfully while maximizing the impact of your event.

1. Understand your budget

    Start with a clear breakdown: Begin by categorizing your budget into clear segments such as venue, catering, technology, entertainment, marketing, and miscellaneous expenses. This clarity helps in allocating funds more effectively and identifying areas where costs can be optimized.

    Monitor regularly: Constantly review your budget as the event planning progresses to help you catch any overspending early and adjust other segments accordingly.

2. Utilize information to scale solutions

    Collaborate with agencies: Use your budget parameters as a tool to guide agencies or vendors. They can tailor their services to fit your budget, providing scaled solutions or alternative options that still meet your event goals.

    Request a menu of options: This menu, provided by each service, empowers you to make informed decisions that align with your budget and event objectives.

3. Increase funding through sponsorships

    Identify potential sponsors: Look for businesses and organizations whose target audience aligns with your event attendees. Offer them value through exposure and engagement opportunities.

Create custom sponsorship packages: Develop various sponsorship levels to accommodate different budgets, ensuring that you can attract a wider range of sponsors.

4. Monetize aspects of the event

   Create exclusive content: Offer premium content or experiences for a fee, such as workshops with special guests, VIP meet and greets, or advanced technology demonstrations.

   Sell merchandise: Sell event-themed merchandise as a way to both increase funding and enhance the attendee experience.

5. Implement admission fees for exclusive experiences

   Evaluate the market: Before deciding on an admission fee, research similar events to ensure your pricing is competitive yet reflects the value of the exclusive experience you're offering.

   Communicate value effectively: Make sure potential attendees understand the unique benefits and exclusive experiences they will gain access to, justifying the admission fee.

6. Leverage digital tools for budget management

   Use event management software: There are numerous software options available that can help manage budgets, track spending in real time, and alert you when you're approaching your limits.

   Use digital marketing: Utilize cost-effective digital marketing strategies to promote your event. Social media, email campaigns, and digital partnerships can provide a high return on investment.

7. Negotiate with vendors and venues

Leverage multiple quotes: Obtain multiple quotes for services and use them as leverage in negotiations to ensure you're getting the best value for your money.

Discuss value-adds: Sometimes, reducing costs isn't about cutting services but about enhancing value. Ask vendors what additional services they can provide within your budget.

8. Plan for contingencies

Set aside a contingency fund: Unexpected costs inevitably arise. Allocating a portion of your budget for unforeseen expenses ensures they won't derail your event or its quality.

Stay flexible: Be prepared to adjust your plans and budget allocations as needed. Flexibility can help you navigate challenges without compromising the event's success.

9. Budget feedback and post-event analysis

Gather feedback: Use post-event surveys to gather feedback on what attendees felt was worth the investment and what wasn't.

Analyze spending versus outcome: Review which investments yielded the highest return in terms of attendee satisfaction and event goals. Use this analysis to inform future budgeting decisions.

Adhere to budget constraints while maximizing the value and success of your events. Remember, effective budget management is not just about cutting costs; it's about making smart choices that enhance the overall event experience for all stakeholders and attendees.

PRO TIPS:

- Make the list of "Top Threes" an ongoing part of your planning process; revisit them when weighing the merit of each concept.
- Ensure buy-in of top-three priorities from all stakeholders.
- Think about how to expand budget parameters by designing strategic sponsorship opportunities into your plan.

CHAPTER 4

Research, Explore, Define

TO-DO LIST:

- Identify research that needs to be done in order to fully understand the situation and fulfill your event's purpose. Note anyone you need to consult for expertise.

- Confirm and refine your target audiences and what you need to understand about them to create a successful solution.

- Talk to decision-makers to understand their perspectives and learn what success means to them.

- Expand and hone your strategy document into a creative brief and have stakeholders approve it before you finalize it.

- Establish an intra-team project-tracking system and communication process in advance of the event, giving team members tools to accomplish tasks, loop people in, coordinate agendas, seek approvals and consensus, or flag potential problems.

WHAT IS THE EVENT'S PURPOSE?

Every event seeks an emotional or intellectual connection between people that drives further meaning or action. When people engage emotionally, they build a relationship, ideally one based on trust and resulting in mutual loyalty. When people engage intellectually, they initiate a dialogue that has the potential to extend beyond the confines of the event. By relating to an audience on both an emotional and an intellectual level, you can create an experience that fosters meaningful connections. That's how marketers create brand loyalty, how innovators build community and advance massive change, and how many great brands begin.

The person or organization holding the event wants participants to do something, whether that's "Be more successful," "Vote for me," or "Buy our product." Ask yourself and your team: "What is our higher purpose?" It's the foundation upon which your event plan will be built; it's the subtext of your messaging strategy. What are you offering people that they can't get anywhere else? If your target audience appreciates the unique benefits you deliver, they'll feel rewarded for attending your event.

AUDIENCE ANALYSIS AND ENGAGEMENT STRATEGY

Conduct surveys and interviews, utilizing these tools to gather direct insights from potential attendees. What are their expectations, interests, and professional goals? If you have access to data from previous events, look for trends in attendance, feedback, and engagement levels to identify what worked and what didn't.

Engagement begins long before the event does. Creating a strategy to attract and maintain interest is crucial. Take advantage of multichannel marketing, from social media to email campaigns, and use various channels to reach your audience where they are most active. Produce engaging content that resonates with your audience's needs and interests.

Think beyond promotional material to informative, valuable content that benefits your audience. Consider pre-event interactive webinars, Q&A sessions, or social media contests to spark interest and participation in advance.

How you deliver your content is as important as the content itself. Engagement architecture is about designing the event's structure to best deliver your messages across multiple interactions. Structure your message and engagement frameworks with your audience in mind, with a content flow that outlines everything you want to communicate during the course of the event. Content flow should align with your audience's needs and how you want them to feel or act as the event unfolds. Consider the mix of keynote speeches, workshops, networking sessions, and other formats that cater to your audience's preferences and learning styles.

A personalized event experience can significantly impact attendee satisfaction and engagement. Gather preferences early by using registration forms that ask about interests, dietary restrictions, or session preferences. Tailor content and recommendations based on attendee data, and customize the event experience by suggesting specific sessions, introductions to like-minded attendees, or personalized schedules.

Try incorporating behavioral science and psychology insights to drive engagement. Understanding the psychological underpinnings of your audience's behavior can enhance outcomes. Use behavioral cues, designing your event to include elements that subtly guide attendees toward your desired outcome, such as networking, learning, or making a purchase. Use principles like scarcity (limited seats for a workshop), authority (expert speakers), or community (group discussions) to motivate attendees.

Be clear on what behavior or outcome you're driving toward and how you'll recognize it. Whether it's increased product knowledge, networking, or direct sales, know what success looks like. Determine in advance how you will evaluate these behaviors: Is it participation in certain sessions, social media engagement, or direct feedback? Establish how you will view and measure the success of your engagement and personalization efforts.

- **Pre-event and post-event surveys:** Measure changes in perception, knowledge, or intentions.

- **Engagement metrics:** Track registrations, attendance rates, session participation, and use of interactive elements.

- **Behavioral data:** Use app check-ins, session selections, and feedback forms to gather data on attendee preferences and behaviors.

Creating memorable and impactful events requires a deep understanding of your audience. It's not just about planning; it's about engaging, understanding, and ultimately driving the desired outcomes through strategic execution. Leverage audience insights for exceptional event design and execution, helping you significantly enhance the impact and success of your event. Understanding and engaging your audience at a deeper level helps ensure that their expectations are met and fosters a memorable experience that prompts your desired behavioral outcomes.

Because several distinct types of audiences may simultaneously be drawn to any given event, think about each of these groups as a persona—an invented character who represents the needs, expectations, and worldview of that audience. Your event's personas will be unique to that event and its goals, which is why you should involve your Renaissance team in thinking through the definitions of these personas.

DEFINING YOUR TARGET AUDIENCE PERSONAS

Based on your research, develop detailed personas for your typical attendees and for different segments of your audience, helping you tailor every aspect of the event to their preferences. Include their professional background, interests, and what they aim to gain from attending your event.

Most people attend a trade show, event, conference, meeting, or expo for a combination of learning, networking, enjoying the experience itself, and to engage in commerce. To build appropriate personas for each of your target audiences, consider each one and ask yourself why they're attending the event. At health care events, for example, certain attendees expect to leave with a medical recertification required by their practice (anything else gained from the event is just a bonus.) Someone attending a cosplay event is probably there for the experience but may also enjoy networking or buying branded merchandise to wear on the plane ride home.

A FRAMEWORK FOR THINKING ABOUT ATTENDEES

The personas that make sense for your event will be uniquely your own. But it also helps to sort attendee needs according to the four basic reasons for attending an event:

- They want to learn something and perhaps fulfill certification requirements.

- They want to network and celebrate with a like-minded community.

- They want to engage in commerce and conduct business.

- They want to have fun and be entertained.

People always attend for some combination of these four reasons.

Seek out data-based insights regarding the primary motivation and tertiary interests that characterize your event's attendees, and note differences between personas. Data helps inform how the event should be orchestrated and its content delivered. Data-based insights also help your team understand who should be assigned to various aspects of the event and where additional expertise will be needed.

Creating detailed personas helps ensure that every aspect of the event is tailored to meet the needs and preferences of your audience, leading to a more engaging and successful event. We've gathered some of the essential steps in building useful event attendee personas for your team's use.

1. Research and gather data

    Begin by gathering as much data as possible about past and potential attendees. Include surveys, social media analytics, previous event feedback, and any available demographic data. You want to know who your attendees are in terms of demographics, professional background, preferences, and interests. Generational differences can make a big difference when choosing everything from menu offerings to guest speakers.

    - **Personalization by permission:** Offer opt-in/opt-out opportunities through an attendee's mobile device. This becomes the interface connecting to the event through sensors (motion detectors, cameras, beacons, QR codes, etc.), which will tell you useful things about what attendees are doing. With this highly specific data applied to your personas, you can go into full personalization.

    - **Make intelligent recommendations:** Tips that are intelligent and personal (the opposite of spam messages) will be well received by attendees, who will love the useful assistance. Deliver information in whatever format the persona prefers or is most useful for them (for example, a proximity-sensing alert that directs them to the nearest exhibit of specific interest).

2. Segment your audience

    Divide your audience into segments based on your research findings. Common segmentation criteria include professional level (e.g., entry-level, mid-career, executives), industry category, tastes, accomplishments, behaviors, motivations, and previous attendance habits. Segmentation, the cornerstone of personalized event planning, allows you to identify distinct groups within your larger audience, each with its own set of characteristics and preferences. Here's how to refine this process.

- **Utilize behavioral data:** Beyond basic demographics, incorporate behavioral data such as previous event attendance, engagement levels (e.g., session attendance, app interactions), and feedback. This helps identify patterns and preferences within your audience.

- **Consider psychographics:** Look at attitudes, aspirations, and other psychological criteria. What drives your attendees beyond professional interests? This can significantly impact how you design your event's content and activities.

- **Leverage technology:** Use data analytics tools and CRM (customer relationship management) software to analyze attendee data more effectively. These tools can help uncover hidden patterns and segment your audience with greater precision.

3. Develop detailed personas

For each audience segment, develop a realistic, multifaceted, detailed persona. A persona is a fictional, composite representation embodying the characteristics of your target segment. Provide in-depth information from many angles to build out the profile of each persona.

- **Professional background:** Include detailed job roles, industry sectors, career milestones, and professional challenges. Understanding the professional landscape of your personas helps in selecting relevant speakers and content.

- **Educational background:** Note their level of education, areas of study, and any continuing education pursuits, helping to guide the complexity and depth of the event's educational offerings.

- **Personal interests:** Dive into hobbies, passions, and non-work-related activities. Events that acknowledge the whole person can foster a deeper connection and engagement.

- **Event goals:** Learn all you can about what they aim to gain from attending your event, such as learning opportunities, networking, or professional development.

- **Their story:** For each persona, create a narrative that includes their professional journey, challenges they face, and what success looks like to them. This story should inform how you structure your event to meet their needs.

- **Goals and pain points:** What specific outcomes does each persona hope to achieve by attending your event? What challenges are they hoping to overcome? Understanding these can guide the selection of keynote speakers, workshop topics, and networking opportunities.

- **Visualized persona:** Create visual representations of your personas. This can include mock social media profiles, avatars, or even mood boards that reflect their professional and personal interests. Visuals can help your planning team empathize with and keep your personas top-of-mind during the planning process.

4. Identify motivations and interests

Understanding why each persona is attending your event and what they're interested in outside of their professional life can help you tailor the event experience. To gain this understanding:

- Conduct surveys or interviews with potential attendees.

- Analyze data from previous events for trends and patterns.

- Consider secondary research sources, like industry reports or social media trends, relevant to your audience.

5. Note differences between personas

It's important to recognize and note the differences between your personas, especially in terms of their primary motivations and tertiary interests. This will help in customizing the event experience for each segment. For example, while some attendees might prioritize networking opportunities, others may prefer educational sessions or workshops.

- **Map the attendee journey:** Consider the entire event experience from an attendee's perspective. Identify key touch points where their motivations and interests can best be addressed. This might include personalized agendas, targeted networking sessions, or interactive workshops.

- **Employ advanced analytics:** Use advanced data analytics to identify trends and patterns in attendee behavior. This can include sentiment analysis of feedback, heat maps of event space engagement, and predictive analytics to forecast future attendee preferences.

- **Create feedback loops:** Implement real-time feedback mechanisms during your event to gauge attendee reactions to sessions, speakers, and overall event design.

Use this data to make on-the-fly adjustments and plan for future events.

6. Use personas to tailor event planning

Use persona information to tailor every aspect of your event-planning process, from the choice of speakers and session topics to networking opportunities and types of entertainment. You'll be taking steps toward creating an event that feels personalized and relevant to each attendee segment.

- **Customized content delivery:** Use technology to deliver personalized content to attendees based on their interests and goals. This could include personalized event schedules, recommended sessions, and targeted networking opportunities.

- **Dynamic session planning:** Plan sessions that adapt to the varied interests of your personas. Consider offering a range of formats (e.g., workshops, panels, 1:1 coaching) to cater to different learning and networking preferences.

- **Engagement beyond the event:** Keep your personas engaged before, during, and after the event. This can include pre-event resources, live polls and Q&A during sessions, and post-event follow-ups that are tailored to each persona's interests and goals.

7. Iterate and refine personas

Personas aren't static. As planning progresses and you gather more data from event registrations, interactions, and feedback, refine your personas to ensure they remain accurate and relevant. This iterative process allows you to continuously tailor and improve the event experience for your attendees.

By focusing on these expanded aspects of persona development, you'll create deeply personalized experiences that resonate with every attendee. This approach enhances the event for attendees while driving higher engagement, satisfaction, and loyalty.

PHASE 1 ADVICE

- Double-check everything and look it over with a fresh eye. Avoid making assumptions.

- Last year's plan is the place from which you can improve. Review notes from debrief sessions that point toward necessary improvements.

- Stay open to all possibilities to create a memorable, engaging experience. Refine as you move forward.

- Reduce intimidation caused by the scope of the plan by breaking things down into smaller steps.

- Everyone brings something different and valuable to the plan. Be inclusive and encourage each member of the team to have their say.

REVISIT THE STRATEGY DOCUMENT AND BUILD A CREATIVE BRIEF

Review the research you've conducted, share the details about your event's attendee personas with the whole team, and meet to discuss how your understanding of the opportunity has changed as a result.

- With your strategy document in hand, brainstorm alterations to the event plan based on any new understandings of the situation. Be sure you are pursuing your biggest potential opportunities.

- Ensure that the full scope of opportunities has been considered and articulated, all key insights or challenges have been captured, and you've considered what's missing (e.g., are any points too vague, can anyone find holes in the plan, or are any choices just a lazy repeat of last year?) before you move on from this step.

- Confirm your highest-priority audience personas and what you want them to think, feel, believe, and do. With that in mind, reconfirm your top three objectives.

- If the event occurs annually or more frequently, or if it focuses on a series of product launches, think in terms of its life cycle. Does it get media coverage in its sector? Is it buzzworthy? Is it time for a transformation? Branding, signage, and graphics are only part of the answer. Dig into shifts in audience interest and relevance.

- Evolve your strategy document into a creative brief (detailed in more depth later in this chapter). This new document will specify more explicitly the goals, insights, steps, and deliverables that will become the actual event plan.

- The strategy team will hand off the creative brief to the creative and design team. Communicate clearly how every team member will approach the next phase of event planning. Document this approach, then share and confirm it with your stakeholders.

As the strategy for your event unfolds and is captured in the creative brief, certain "must-haves" will surface. Common challenges at this stage often include finding more "want-to-haves" than even a preliminary budget will allow, and a lack of consensus or clarity among decision-makers regarding which event features are actually essential. Press decision-makers to articulate their priorities; what seems like a lack of clarity may be a lack of solidarity or an indication of dissent. Address challenges and preempt future misdirection by hosting a Scenarios Methodology session.

THE SCENARIOS METHODOLOGY

The Scenarios Methodology is a proven research tool used to offer stakeholders a wide range of creative approaches and induce them to identify the biggest priorities and challenges of each approach. This methodology can actually help strengthen the relationships between everyone involved, ensuring the success of the event. The agency's strategist typically facilitates the session while someone captures the notes. Here's what's involved:

Develop a series of creative scenarios for the event plan based on what you've learned so far. Each scenario is a sketch of a creative vision, not a fully realized concept, that you will present to decision-makers at the session. Make each scenario as different from the others as possible, designed to force choices around areas that need clarity.

For example, assume that at the event's big networking bash, guests will be served dinner. One scenario is an elegant affair with fine table linens, thematic centerpieces, uniformed servers, assigned seating, and a menu featuring gourmet selections named to echo key experiences from the event. Another scenario features an outdoor dinner party with food trucks, a band, games, string lights, and picnic tables under a tent. Another scenario might take participants through a progressive dinner at multiple eateries around the city. As invented scenarios, not actual recommendations, you can be as specific or as outrageous as you like. Your goal is to observe and record responses to each concept. Create as many scenarios as you need, designed to drive key decisions. Represent each scenario (perhaps on posters hung around the room) and ask participants to rank them (perhaps with colored stickers), allowing some ideas to rise to the top and others to fall to the bottom. Ask participants why they voted as they did. Why did they prefer some ideas to others? Listen for true priorities and objectives and for anything surprising, new, or unexpected. Invite people to respond to the results of the vote. Do upvotes indicate a need to reshuffle elements from various scenarios? Is anyone interested in resubmitting their votes after hearing their colleagues?

The Scenarios Methodology gets disparate groups talking, reveals new information about an organization's needs and priorities, and gives the facilitator a chance to understand various concerns, address them, and drive agreement regarding what's absolutely essential. It reduces costs by focusing the creative development scope early in the process. It can also create a sense of empathy and trust as people struggle together to make the event the best it can be. Make sure you're taking a fresh approach and fully articulating any new opportunities. The information you present in your creative brief shapes everything that follows. It will never be less expensive to make an adjustment than it is at this point in the process.

BUILDING AN EFFECTIVE CREATIVE BRIEF

The first sentence or two of your creative brief for the event should capture the essence of the challenge and its opportunities for effecting positive, lasting change. The start of your creative brief should serve as a rallying cry that makes everyone on the team want to be a part of making the event a success. Everything that follows should be driven by these opening statements crafted to bring clarity and purpose to the creative process. These opening statements can also refer to your vision of what *beautiful* looks like or to the possibilities to be realized when the event is a success.

Note thought-provoking ideas, concepts, or challenges that are specific to key event goals, and ask questions that help turn them into productive solutions. For example, if one of your audience personas is a large contingent of return attendees, how can you engage their fond memories of past events while giving them something new and delightful to remember from this event? If one of your top three objectives is engaging the audience so they become social media ambassadors, how might you orchestrate the entire three-day event to create must-share moments? If one of your top three objectives is to increase revenue, what kind of experience might attract new sponsorships?

Begin work on your creative brief by thoroughly reviewing the approved strategy document. Identify and extract core insights, strategic goals, and the event's primary objective. These insights will serve as the foundation of your creative brief. Then follow these steps to build an amazing, unique, effective creative brief.

- **Define the event's objective clearly:** Translate your approved strategy document into a clear, concise objective for the event. This objective statement should include what the event aims to achieve, such as raising awareness, driving donations, or engaging a specific community.

    - Make sure the objective aligns with the broader goals outlined in the strategy document.

    - Include a concise summary of the event strategy, focusing on its key elements. This summary should include the event's target audience, main objectives, key messages, and desired outcomes as outlined in the strategy document.

    - Clearly state the purpose of the creative brief within the document. This statement should directly relate to how the brief will guide the creative and planning process for the event, emphasizing the transformation of strategic objectives into creative execution.

- **Identify the target audience:** Specify your target audience. Describe the demographic and psychographic profiles of the target audience, including age, interests, behaviors, and any other relevant characteristics. Understanding the audience is crucial for tailoring the event's messaging and design to meet their preferences and needs. We go into greater depth and detail on this item later in this chapter.

- **Outline key messages:** Based on the strategy document, distill the key messages that need to be communicated throughout the event. These messages should be impactful, easy to understand, and directly tied to the event's objectives. Consider how these messages will be woven into various aspects of the event, from marketing materials to the event's programming.

- **Detail the creative concept:** Develop a creative concept that will bring the event to life. This concept should be innovative and align with the event's objectives, key messages, and target audience.

  - Describe how the concept will be visualized through design elements, thematic elements, and the overall event experience.

  - Articulate the creative challenge that the brief aims to address. This involves translating the strategic objectives into a specific creative question or problem the team needs to solve through the event's design, messaging, and execution.

  - Ensure that the brief references the brand guidelines that need to be adhered to. This section ensures that all creative executions are consistent with the brand's identity and messaging framework.

  - Offer high-level creative direction based on the strategic document's insights. This should inspire the creative team but not limit their creativity, and could include mood boards, themes, or conceptual ideas that align with your strategic goals.

- **Specify communication channels and tactics:** List the channels and tactics you'll use to promote the event and engage with the audience. This could include social media, email marketing, PR, and on-the-ground activities. Detail how each channel will be used to communicate the event's key messages effectively.

- **Highlight logistic considerations:** Even though a creative brief focuses on the creative aspect, including a section on logistic considerations (like venue, timing, required technology) ensures that the creative concepts are realistic and feasible to execute.

- **Set creative milestones and deadlines:** Establish a timeline for the creative process, including key milestones and deadlines for each phase of event planning. This helps track progress and ensures that the creative team and event planners are aligned. List the specific creative deliverables expected from the brief, ranging from branding elements, marketing materials, and digital content, to the event's thematic design. Provide clear descriptions and the purpose of each deliverable.

- **Incorporate feedback mechanisms:** Plan for regular check-ins and revisions based on feedback from the team and other stakeholders. This ensures that the creative brief remains a living document that adapts to new insights or changes in strategy.

- **Define metrics for success:** Link back to the event's objectives by defining how success will be measured. Include both qualitative and quantitative metrics, such as attendee satisfaction, media coverage, social media engagement, and any other relevant KPIs. Translate the strategic success metrics into creative benchmarks to help evaluate the effectiveness of the creative elements in achieving the event's objectives.

- **Foster collaboration and inspiration:** Encourage the team to use the creative brief as a source of inspiration and a foundation for collaboration. The brief should be a tool that invites creative thinking, problem solving, and team alignment toward the common goal of making the event a success.

- **Finalize and distribute:** Once the creative brief is complete, ensure it is reviewed for alignment with the strategy document. Make sure you've defined the audience personas, top three objectives, and scope of the opportunity accurately, while delineating challenges the larger team must address in subsequent planning sessions. Finalize the brief and distribute it to your team, event planners, managers, decision-makers, and other key stakeholders for implementation.

By following these steps, the event-planning team can ensure that their creative brief aligns with the approved strategy document and provides clear, actionable guidance for translating strategic insights into compelling and effective creative executions.

PRO TIPS:

- To validate the brand relevance of the purpose statement included in the creative brief, substitute the names of other events, associations, or brands. If it works for them, it may not be authentic or specific enough to represent your event's unique opportunity.

- Agencies should conduct a proactive blue-sky session with their core team to explore opportunities for providing client services beyond the contractual scope of work. Offering strong, strategic ideas can be an effective way to build the relationship, demonstrate value, and elevate the long-term effectiveness of the event.

IMPLEMENT A PROJECT-TRACKING SYSTEM

Once your creative brief is developed, vetted, and finalized, you'll want to implement a project-tracking system to enable your team to function at a high-performance level. Begin with a list of known deliverables laid out against a timeline in a table that indicates key information, including who is accountable, the status of the deliverable (in progress, delayed, on time, etc.), what needs to happen for progress to continue (budget approval, contingency plans, etc.), along with an obvious way to flag anything in jeopardy or to alert key team members to take action.

- Use the project-tracking system to help with the heavy lifting

- Define the deliverables that you will produce.

- Review and revise the timeline based on the most recent developments.

- Review the team composition and roles and responsibilities, making any necessary adjustments.

- Review the budget and revise the estimate of available funds.

- Define a collaborative workspace within the online system where everyone can post and access critical information.

- Develop the communication plan that all team members will adhere to (team meeting schedule, individual deliverables, timeline, and budget guidance.)

Of the many professional project-tracking systems, the best one for you may be the one that most of your team is familiar with. Because most companies invest in one specific system or rely on proprietary systems, many agencies stay fluent in multiple systems. These tend to be Cloud-based/online platforms everyone can access with the right security measures in place. Whatever your platform or method, ensure that everyone agrees on how to track progress, assure accountability, and immediately recognize any changes or delays so other areas affected can adjust or respond.

Choose a system that all team members can access, and that one person (usually a project manager or producer) oversees, keeping it updated and ready for any changes to be reviewed at your weekly event status meetings. Ideally, the project-tracking system exists in the same Cloud space where all event assets and documents will be stored.

- **Choosing the right project-tracking tool:** Look for a tool that fits the scale of your event, offers customization, and is user friendly. Research and compare different project management software. Evaluate features like task assignment, deadline tracking, and real-time collaboration. Opt for a tool with strong mobile support to ensure team members can update and check in on the go.

- **Customizing the project-tracking tool:** Tailor the tool to precisely fit the needs and workflow of your event-planning process. Create a project template that reflects the main phases of your event planning (e.g., pre-planning, logistics, execution). Set up custom fields for budget tracking, vendor contacts, and venue details. Use labels, tags, or color coding to categorize tasks by department, urgency, or completion status.

- **Training the team:** Ensure every team member can effectively utilize the project-tracking tool. Organize a training session to walk through the tool's features and best practices. Create a quick-reference guide or cheat sheet that team members can refer to. Encourage team members to practice using the tool with mock tasks and scenarios.

- **Establishing a task-management system:** Break down the event into actionable tasks and milestones. Define major milestones (e.g., venue booking, vendor contracts) and break them down into smaller tasks. Assign tasks to specific team members with clear deadlines. Monitor progress through the tool, and adjust assignments and deadlines as needed.

- **Integrating deadline alerts and reminders:** Keep the team on track with automated notifications. Set up email or app notifications for upcoming deadlines and overdue tasks. Utilize calendar integrations to visualize the timeline of the event-planning process. Encourage team members to set personal reminders for critical deadlines.

- **Facilitating real-time collaboration:** Enhance communication and collaboration among the team. Use the tool's commenting and discussion features to keep communication about tasks in one place. Share files and documents directly within the tool to ensure everyone has access to the latest versions. Schedule regular virtual check-ins using the tool's meeting or integration features.

- **Monitoring and reporting progress:** Provide visibility into the event's planning status and address any issues promptly. Use the tool's dashboard and reporting features to create status reports. Regularly review project progress in team meetings, highlighting achievements and addressing challenges. Adjust the plan based on progress reports to stay on track or address any delays.

By meticulously selecting, customizing, and utilizing a project-tracking tool, event-planning teams can significantly enhance their efficiency and effectiveness. This comprehensive approach not only ensures that tasks are completed on time but also fosters a collaborative and transparent work environment, paving the way for successful event execution.

PRO TIPS:

- The best project-tracking system is the one everyone on the team is willing to use from the first day.

PHASE 2

DESIGN THE PLAN

- Collaborate to explore innovative ideas that solve your challenges.

- Sketch, prototype, test, and refine your approach.

- Improve sustainability.

- Make use of a comprehensive event services shopping list.

- Build sponsorship programs.

- Consider your virtual/digital event objectives; integrate that into the event plan.

- Craft a plan with solutions feasible to execute that meet your objectives.

- Get this plan approved.

- Plus: Explore special insights for exhibitors to optimize the opportunity and exhibit space.

Phase 2 brings the opportunity to think big, consider every option, and then focus your time, talent, and resources to tighten and finalize the event plan. Time spent in refining the design details will save money when it's time to build.

CHAPTER 5

Designing Your Event Plan

TO-DO LIST:

- Review the creative brief, deliverables, timeline, and budget within the team.

- Meet to brainstorm ideas with the entire team, exploring innovative approaches to any challenges.

- Evaluate the ideas that best reflect your top three objectives and best suit your creative brief. Identify the most promising ideas and explore in greater depth how they might work.

- Design eco-aware sustainability features into your event plan.

- Demonstrate how the opportunities you offer help sponsors and their intended audiences. Nurture sponsors at all levels to build a pipeline of sponsors for the future.

- Secure executive approval and consensus at key inflection points before moving forward.

IMAGINE WAYS TO MEET YOUR GOALS AND OBJECTIVES

You've done the homework; now it's time to design the event plan. Arrange a meeting for the core team to present your creative brief to the brainpower of your Renaissance team (some of whom won't stay on as work progresses). Send a copy of the creative brief to everyone on the team prior to this first meeting, so they can review it and arrive familiar with the information and ready to contribute (especially critical if some or all of the team is participating remotely). Engage everyone in sessions to brainstorm, challenge, and refine concepts and solutions that address each of the opportunities and challenges articulated in the brief. Inspire innovative thinking, speak to your purpose, and think about the future—for the event, for the organization, for your team. Visualize opportunities, answer questions, and assign roles. People may choose to divide and conquer, solve for specialized aspects of a challenge, then regroup to compare results and map out next steps.

Review the key insights articulated in the creative brief, your top three lists, and your audience personas. Challenge the team to solve all open issues with solutions addressing the needs of each audience persona. Allow the most relevant team member to lead discussions, depending on the issue or its solution. For example, if you work with a data analysis expert, you'll want them in the room if you're asking the team to integrate data-capture opportunities into their creative solutions.

It's important to reiterate any parameters that must be met: timing for the event, space restrictions, general budget guidelines, and any challenging or unique venue opportunities. Limitations often spark creative solutions. Maybe your venue, an older property with low ceilings, actually boasts an interesting history. How can the team leverage that history? Maybe there's troublesome road construction between the venue and the airport. How can your team find a creative solution to remove some of that pain for attendees?

Make sure someone representing the logistics team attends this first meeting and stays in the loop. Specify the ramifications of anything unusual or challenging about the event logistics. If it's straightforward in terms of load-in and load-out requirements, your producer can probably handle it. Don't assume that rules applying to one venue will work for another (they generally don't).

BRAINSTORMING, SKETCHING, E-STORMING, BRAINWRITING, AND ITERATION

Optimize your event through iteration, the process of imagining, testing, and improving on ideas. Brainstorming sessions invite thinking from various people who can then improve on each other's ideas. But some ideas may not be heard because of enthusiasm for one's own ideas or because junior roles may be intimidated by those who outrank them. That's why it's good practice to invite team members to work on their own as well as in groups. Then, invite the entire team to collaborate by combining ideas, validating them against the top threes, and expanding on the strongest concepts.

- **Brainstorming:** Appoint a facilitator to keep the process on track and capture ideas on a whiteboard, flip charts, virtual whiteboard, or someplace where everyone can see them. Set a time limit (perhaps thirty minutes) and ask people to throw out blue-sky ideas. Suspend judgment at this time and invite people to build on each other's ideas. Frame various challenges in fun, thought-provoking ways, a useful technique for soliciting input from those with deep insights or a valuable perspective without requiring them to make any further commitment.

- **E-storming:** After the meeting, message everyone on the team asking them to respond to a specific challenge. The questions you ask may sound like "Describe the attendee journey from the first day to the last," or "What happens the first time someone enters the general session?"

- **Sketching:** A quick way to capture a glimpse of an idea before you lose it, sketching allows you to visualize and share concepts, whether it's a quick line drawing to represent the basic elements of an idea or concept or a sketch created with words, images pulled from the internet, design software, or even a pie chart. Some teams use sketching to break the ice and get people thinking during a group session. Save useful sketches in the group's project management system for later reference or further iteration.

- **Brainwriting:** Ask people to make sketches and bring them to the meeting; then ask everyone to pass their ideas to the right. After two or three minutes, pass again, until everyone has seen every idea. Discuss and note favorite ideas that will be carried forward for further iteration.

NARROW THE FIELD AND EXPAND THE DETAIL

A good leader will know when to stop exploring new ideas and redirect the team's energy to evaluating the ideas on the table based on how well they address the creative brief. Will the experience take participants on a valuable, memorable journey? Are there any weak links in the chain? Did you fail to address an imperative on your Top Threes list? Focus your next work session on fleshing out the most promising ideas.

Vote ideas up or down through discussion, a show of hands, the use of colored stickers that count as votes when applied to concepts posted around the room, or any other narrow-and-nurture process through which only the best (most on-strategy, most innovative, most feasible) ideas go forward.

KILL YOUR DARLINGS

Sound advice (originally given to a writer fighting to protect a favorite bit of prose no longer supporting the narrative) is "kill your darlings." This advice applies to experience design, too. Sometimes we have an idea so amazing, we're tempted to overlook the fact that it's a forced fit. Even if it feels painful, we have to let it go. (A smart creative director will maintain a file of all those great ideas that didn't work; they may work elsewhere.)

For a big project with several venues, a substantial menu of event happenings, and multiple audiences, you may have separate teams focused on various pieces, but bring as many decision-makers into the approval process as you can for this next step. You're working to make sure that everything fits together in a synergistic way. Present your event plan to the event manager and all the decision-makers. Better to seek their input earlier than later. If they raise an objection at this stage, you may be able to answer their concern and save the essential concept. If you wait to ask their approval and they object later on, you may be facing a more painful and expensive scenario. The event manager, account lead, and any other necessary stakeholders should work closely to shepherd the event plan through this stage, make any necessary adjustments, and secure approval before proceeding.

SUSTAINABILITY: ALWAYS A WIN-WIN

Every business concern needs to bring a sustainability plan to the party. It's better for the planet, and it's also good business. Make sure any approved event budget includes practical, measurable sustainability practices. Engage all stakeholders in a green plan from the beginning. Creating a sustainable event isn't just about being environmentally conscious—it's also a strategic approach to attract sponsors, enhance brand reputation, and ensure the longevity of your events. Prioritizing eco-conscious choices makes a difference.

Provide clear guidelines and tips on reducing waste. Be as specific as possible to let exhibitors and attendees understand what to expect. Demonstrate how following your guidelines will save money and protect the reputations of all involved.

- **Engage your community.** Once you've communicated your sustainability goals, it's easier to encourage exhibitors and sponsors to choose from the menu you present.

- **Offer rental choices.** Items purchased for exhibits and sponsorship activations are often left behind or discarded. Offer a selection of high-quality rental furniture and display structures that can be returned and reused at the end of the show. Make sure the suppliers recycle rental pieces at the end of their usable life. Also make sure that all fabric drape is recycled and repurposed.

- **Encourage donations.** Many materials that are loaded into the venue can be repurposed if someone plans ahead of time to find these items a good home. Arrange to reduce waste by setting up donation programs that send unused supplies or materials to local charities.

- **Use eco-friendly print and fabrication materials.** Plan to use print items (such as giveaways, graphics, and leaflets) without dates or show locations so leftovers can be repurposed for future events. Make sure all single-use rigid graphics are printed on recyclable substrates. Avoid polystyrene, which contains chemicals that are harmful to the environment and slow to degrade. Print signs on 100 percent recyclable paper using only non-VOC inks.

- **Reward green actions.** Promote the sustainability efforts of partners and exhibitors as part of the messaging in your event communications plan. Create win-win opportunities for your partners to boost their brand by publicly demonstrating their commitment to sustainability through your programs.

- **Green up the show floor.** Engaging local union labor in your sustainability process will help reduce waste and even help with travel costs (and transportation emissions). Explain your sustainability protocols and provide the training and tools to execute them. Distribute plenty of recycling bins on the show floor, and make sure everyone on the team understands the plan to deal with waste in a responsible manner.

- **Walk the talk.** Carpeting is ubiquitous at trade shows and expositions, but it doesn't need to be. By eliminating aisle carpeting from the expo hall, the benefits can really add up. It saves transportation of all that heavy cargo and keeps all the tape, plastic coverings, and loads of materials out of landfills. Progressive agencies offer a carbon calculator that can help you promote how many tons of emissions are saved for every unused square foot of carpet. If you must have carpeting, talk to your vendor and make sure they offer reused and/or recyclable options, including padding made from recycled materials.

- **Digitize to energize sustainability efforts.** Instead of printing handouts, catalogs, pricing sheets, and such, offer to distribute materials electronically. Digital practices offer a range of benefits: minimizing impact by reducing carbon emissions from shipping materials; reducing the amount of paper used; reducing trash generated from discarded materials; major reductions in labor costs, shipping costs, storage space, and material-handling fees; easier tracking of and follow up for lead-generation data; and unlike printed pieces, it's easy and quick to fix errors or make changes to digital content, even mid-event. (A good rule of thumb is to only print giveaway materials that are of such high quality and long-term relevance that they will be valued and not discarded.)

- **Use energy-efficient tactics.** Think about all aspects of your event along the supply chain that draw power, create emissions, or produce waste. Use energy-efficient equipment whenever available and establish a power-down policy so that all AV equipment is turned off overnight when possible.

- **Work with vendors and venues already prioritizing the environment.** Don't be found guilty by association with bad players; learn about the green practices your partners are already using and build your plan together.

- **Establish a more sustainable transportation strategy.** Over-the-road shipping should be done using trucks qualified as EPA SmartWay certified. You can also enforce policies to reduce engine idling on-site.

- **Lead by example.** Encourage people to do the right thing by showing them how rewarding it can be. You can be proof that it matters.

Sustainability efforts are most effective when they are designed into the plan. Consider some of these tips for reducing waste and promoting sustainability at events.

- **Highlight sustainability in your event plan:** Clearly outline your sustainability goals and practices in your event plan and in any sponsorship proposals. Show potential sponsors how their brand aligns with these values.

- **Choose eco-friendly materials:** Opt for biodegradable, recyclable, or reusable materials for event branding, signage, and decorations. Share this commitment with potential sponsors and include it in exhibitor kits.

- **Waste-reduction plan:** Develop a comprehensive plan to minimize event waste. Include strategies for food waste, recycling, and composting. Sponsors are keen to associate with events that demonstrate a commitment to waste reduction.

- **Water conservation measures:** Implement water-saving practices, such as offering water stations instead of bottled water. This can be an attractive point for sponsors focused on environmental sustainability.

- **Sustainable catering options:** Choose caterers who use locally sourced, organic, and seasonal produce. This not only supports local businesses but also reduces the carbon footprint associated with food transportation.

- **Encourage public transportation and carpooling:** Promote the use of public transport, carpooling, or even provide shuttle services to reduce the event's carbon footprint. Sponsors interested in reducing emissions will find this appealing.

- **Carbon offset programs:** Offer or encourage participants and sponsors to contribute to carbon offset programs to balance out the event's carbon footprint.

- **Eco-friendly swag:** Choose sustainable promotional items and merchandise, such as products made from recycled materials or items that are attractive, useful, and long-lasting.

- **Green certifications for events:** Work toward obtaining a green certification for your event, such as ISO 20121. This can significantly boost your event's attractiveness to eco-conscious sponsors.

- **Partner with environmental organizations:** Collaborate with nonprofits focused on sustainability. This partnership can enhance your event's credibility and attract sponsors aligned with environmental causes.

- **Showcase green technologies:** Integrate and showcase green technologies at your event, such as solar-powered charging stations. This can attract tech-savvy sponsors interested in innovation.

- **Sustainable event merchandising:** Offer merchandise that is ethically sourced or made from sustainable materials. This is a growing interest area for sponsors and attendees alike.

continued

- **Highlight local sustainability efforts:** Showcase local sustainability initiatives or projects at your event, connecting sponsors with community efforts and local impact.

- **Virtual event components:** Incorporate virtual elements to reduce travel-related emissions. This can expand your event's reach and attract sponsors interested in global accessibility.

- **Sustainability reporting:** Commit to measuring and reporting on your event's sustainability performance. Transparent reporting can build trust with sponsors.

- **Eco-friendly venue features:** If the venue is predetermined, highlight its sustainable features or improvements made for the event. This demonstrates a proactive approach to sustainability.

- **Involve sponsors in green initiatives:** Encourage sponsors to participate in or even lead sustainability workshops, talks, or activities during the event.

- **Energy conservation campaigns:** Launch campaigns or initiatives aimed at conserving energy during the event (this can be a unique selling point for sponsors).

- **Reduce, reuse, recycle:** Emphasize a strong commitment to "the three Rs" in all aspects of event planning, from stage design to attendee gifts.

- **Green event awards:** Recognize and award sponsors and participants who contribute significantly to the event's sustainability goals, fostering a culture of green competition.

- **Sustainable transportation for event staff and participants:** Arrange for sustainable transportation options for everyone involved in the event, further reducing its carbon footprint.

- **Use of sustainable technologies in event production:** Implement sustainable technologies in event production, such as using recycled materials for stages and booths.

- **Continuous improvement and feedback loop:** After the event, gather feedback on sustainability practices, and look for areas of improvement. Share these insights with sponsors and participants to demonstrate your commitment to continuous improvement in sustainability.

By incorporating these tips into your event planning and clearly communicating them to potential sponsors and attendees, you can create a compelling proposition that aligns with the growing demand for sustainable practices in the business and event-planning sectors. This practice helps position the event organizer as a leader in sustainability, enhances the brand's reputation, and makes a positive impact on the environment.

OUTLINE YOUR EVENT FLOW AND BUILD YOUR EVENT PLAN

An event is so much more than a cool theme or high-profile presenters. Your event is the sum total of thousands of touch points, each of which can add to or detract from its success. Outline a step-by-step flow of how the ideas work together to create the event and offer a unified experience for participants. Create sketches or prototypes if they're relevant. Do more research if it's needed. Take field trips to further explore ideas. When you're ready, build out a detailed plan orchestrating the way various experiences flow together in a journey for participants, working to uncover any unexpected challenges that need to be solved. Think of it as an experience map, with a customized path for each audience persona.

> Your event is so much more than a cool theme or high-profile presenters. Your event is the sum total of thousands of touch points, each of which can add to or detract from its success.

Pre-event communications plan: List details about any marketing materials that are planned for pre-event engagement, including invitations, promotions, advertising, and the event website. Identify how you're reaching out to exhibitors, sponsors, and various audience personas. Think about the cadence of these communications—does it engage the audience in useful, relevant ways? Will you survey your exhibitors and guests, and what do you hope to learn?

The event plan: Create a step-by-step outline of the attendee journey based on your approved concept. Put yourselves in the shoes of the event attendees. Eventually you'll want to do this for each audience persona, noting any important differences. List every point of engagement with a description of the experience.

- What's their travel experience?
- When do they first engage with the event app?
- Are they greeted at the hotel?
- What happens when they arrive at the venue?
- What are their engagement choices?

Add sketches created during your brainstorming sessions. Make a special note of new features and areas that require further research or investigation. Highlight the most exciting or significant things happening each day. Do this exercise for each day of the event, tracking places where experiences differ for remote attendees. Note opportunities for in-person attendees and virtual participants to network and collaborate.

Consider how the event closes; note the memorable moments you're creating and want to reinforce, so each attendee leaves feeling inspired and grateful they could attend. Indicate how you'll capture attendee feedback (as appropriate) at key touch points.

Post-event plan: Many event managers stay in touch with their audience on a year-round basis as part of their larger marketing plan. Specific to this event, indicate any planned messaging or surveys designed to reinforce the event experience and learn from it. Plan ahead to ask participants what they thought about various aspects of the experience, helping you understand where you delivered value and where you can improve next year.

Outlining the event plan helps you see what you've got to work with, while recognizing what's missing. Is there an audience persona you don't sufficiently understand? Will you deploy technology you've never used?

Use fieldwork to immerse your team in firsthand experiences related to the event that can inspire new perspectives for solutions. Field trips help deliver accurate, comprehensive inputs for project design and minimize last-minute "I never knew that" surprises. Conduct field studies anytime an idea needs to be validated. Consider multiple, quick visits rather than long ones. For example, if your event relates to the food industry, visit farmers, bakers, chefs. Interview grocery store managers and observe how shoppers experience the products on display. Think about your audience personas. Are they library users? Museum goers? Flip-flop wearers? A field trip teaches you about the people you hope to connect with and helps you personalize each experience.

To get the most value out of your field trip:

- Make sure a representative selection of team members participates so you can benefit from different perspectives.

- Arrange to go with guides who really know their stuff. Seek answers from the experts.

- Document your field trip by taking photos and recording notes. Share your images and insights with the team.

- Look for opportunities to solve problems for your audience personas. Discuss with your team.

ORCHESTRATION

It's easy to think of an event in terms of a static series of happenings, but experienced event planners view events as a continuum, a meaningful experience that evolves over time and propels the attendee along an inviting, relevant, personalized path. Your event plan reveals the story connecting the parts of the experience into a journey.

Think of your event as a piece of orchestral music, a film score. There should be sweet moments, challenges, heart-pounding crescendos, quiet corners. If you're loud all the time, everything just becomes noise. Which voices do you want to hear clearly, at which moments, and when should other voices be heard? You are the conductor of your event.

When you present your event plan for approval, be prepared to demonstrate how each aspect of the event is orchestrated to bring each of your audience personas to the *beautiful* place described in your top three objectives.

PRO TIPS:

- The process of sketching ideas (or "brainwriting"), sharing them in rapid-fire format, and reviewing them in a roundtable is a productive, efficient way to generate ideas and iterate variations.

- Ensure that someone on the team is assigned to maintain solid note taking, especially in client meetings. Document key takeaways and indicate any client responses/approvals and next-step deliverables.

- Look for opportunities to combine two or more activities into a single, stronger activity, eliminating anything extraneous. Identify which concept has the best potential to create a memorable, relevant experience that fulfills your top three objectives. Then run the idea by an extended team of experts inside and outside of your team to validate it.

- Evaluate all aspects of the event plan using the lens of sustainability practice. (Your sponsors and attendees will!)

- Every event plan will have its unique challenges. Stay nimble—the best plans can be disrupted, with new solutions put in place. Evaluate the implications of these changes on the timeline, budget, and workflow. Proactive change involves risk; acknowledge risks in your plan.

CHAPTER 6

Event Services Shopping List

TO-DO LIST:

- Consider everything your event might require. From the basics like catering and audiovisual (AV) equipment to nuanced needs like special permits, safety and security planning, and transportation, envisioning your event in its entirety will help ensure your shopping list covers it all.

- Conduct research on potential service providers. Look for reviews, ratings, and portfolios to gauge their reputation and quality of work. This step is crucial in identifying vendors that align with your event's needs and budget.

- Reach out to short-listed service providers for detailed proposals. Ensure these proposals include specifics such as services offered, contingency planning, pricing, and any additional costs. Comparing proposals side by side will help in making informed decisions.

- Once you've selected your service providers, negotiate terms that best fit your event's needs. Pay close attention to cancellation policies, payment schedules, and any contract clauses that might affect your event's flexibility.

- Finalize agreements with service providers by signing contracts and making any required deposits. This step officially secures their services for your event date.

Each event has its own shopping list, for its own set of requirements and challenges. From the grandest galas to the most intimate events, success hinges on meticulous planning and the careful selection of services that will bring your vision to life. In this chapter, we delve into an array of essential event services, offering insights and guidance to help you curate your perfect event services shopping list. Designed to equip you with the knowledge and tools necessary to make informed decisions, this comprehensive overview can help ensure that your event is memorable and seamless, from start to finish.

EVENT PLANNER CONSIDERATIONS LIST

The job of the event planner is incredibly complex, requiring a mastery of the big picture and management of the smallest details. Every event planner sees their role differently. Their organizations are staffed to do some work internally and hire supplier partners to manage the rest. The following is a comprehensive list of the services that event planners should consider; they may not need everything, but it's a good practice to review first before rejecting or making an assignment.

- **Health and Safety Services**
  - Consulting: Industry experts provide safety assessments and recommendations backed by research, data, and best practices.
  - On-site safety record: Ask about your suppliers' practices regarding safety assurance for load-in crew, staff, and all participants. Ask to see their standard risk-management plan, plus recommendations for an event-specific crisis-management plan. Verify that safety training, incident reporting, and response procedures are part of the standard operating procedure for the general services contractor.

- Event favorability reports: Learn about how current Centers for Disease Control and Prevention (CDC) guidance, local regulations, vaccination rates, etc., apply to your situation.

- Occupancy analysis and traffic flow planning: Get a floor plan detailing the best use of common spaces, learn about helpful technology, and learn other solutions to maximize a safe experience.

- Communications strategy and messaging: Have a plan for communicating and implementing a crisis response, managing on-site issues, and taking a proactive, transparent approach to press materials and talking points.

- Insurance, liability, and risk management: Understand and manage contracts with expectations regarding insurance coverage. Your corporate lawyer is the best resource here, but many organizations can help ensure you've pulled all the necessary permits for your chosen venue and city.

- Security: Whether it's protecting the AV equipment backstage, securing the footpath taken by celebrity guests or entertainers, or keeping patent pending/ trade secret products away from prying eyes, security professionals know all the considerations required to give you confidence.

- **Design and Creative**

  - Activation design: Telling your brand story and thinking about how to take audiences in new directions that inspire learning, joy, connection, and trust.

- Content strategy: Creating, orchestrating, and communicating your message in a way that's aligned visually, verbally, and virtually across all media.

- Exhibit and environmental design: Ensuring your structures, graphics, lighting, and digital displays engage audiences and enrich experiences.

- Experience design: Telling your story through multisensory experiences that engage attendees on an emotional and visceral level.

- Graphic design and production: Signs, screens, banners, and structures must be created in use-specific ways and delivered with flawless production quality.

- Presentation decks, video, and film: Speaker support for presenters, video, and film messages all rely on the keen eye of a designer who knows how to work within AV parameters.

- AR/VR experiences: Augmented and virtual reality experiences can be used to showcase products and services in strategic ways.

- Web design: Informed by digital strategy and created by experts to optimize the user experience.

- **Strategy**

  - Attendee journey: Leveraging every touch point as an engagement opportunity.

  - Audience acquisition strategy: Helping you reach the right audiences and grow attendance year over year.

  - Audience engagement strategy: Knowing what you want audiences to do and designing objective-driven experiences that deliver.

- Brand and message strategy: Ensuring that your brand is consistently represented in ways that are effective, efficient, powerful, and personalized.

- Event portfolio planning: Optimizing your total marketing spend against the key audiences you need to reach and existing events that succeed.

- Event research: Benefiting from what's known about consumer concerns and the most successful event models to plan for the future.

- Growth strategy: Tapping market insights to prioritize key segments that hold the most potential for growth.

- Measurement and analysis: Establishing the key drivers of success and a plan to measure the relative performance of each aspect of the event.

- Sustainability strategy: Event planning that leverages the most effective tools, materials, and technologies to support sustainability goals.

- **Sponsorship**

  - Sponsorship strategy: Data-driven method for creating engaging, exciting sponsor opportunities that also drive value for attendees.

  - Sponsor prospectus creative and design: Smart alignment opportunities, experiential activations, and exhibit designs that inspire sponsor participation.

  - Sponsorship sales: Engaging professionals who know how to increase event revenue while managing and retaining sponsors.

  - Sponsorship management: Supporting and communicating with sponsors, vendors, and exhibitors so everyone performs at peak potential.

- Sponsorship growth and retention: Leveraging a data-informed strategy and reporting system to keep sponsors and to develop new prospects.

- **Event Creator**

  - Overall program management: Soup-to-nuts oversight, generally provided by larger events agencies and GSCs.

  - Customer/exhibitor support: Supporting exhibitors through experienced, helpful support centers that are available as needed via phone, email, text, and at on-site booths from load-in to load-out days.

  - Production services: From lighting design and AV solutions to theatrical extravaganzas, show pros know how to create memorable experiences.

  - Content and speaker management: Educating, entertaining, and inspiring audiences by developing speeches, hiring professionals, and making it look effortless.

  - Graphics: From small collateral pieces to giant digital displays, your event requires a professional look and fcel.

  - Show site services: Managing everything that happens at the venue, from installation to dismantling, including electrical services, material handling, furnishings, and everything it takes to keep the event running smoothly.

  - Talent acquisition and management: Contracting keynote speakers, dancers, bands, and other entertainers requires professional attention to contracts, expectations, and implications for staging and equipment.

- Venue selection: Identifying event spaces chosen specifically to accommodate and amplify your event's objectives.

- Space allocation: Assess and understand the best use and design of available space for all activations, keynote, exhibits, breakouts, etc.

- Food and beverage (F&B): Determine the scale of meal service desired (banquet, catered, craft services), and negotiate how services will be provided and at what cost. Many venues maintain exclusive contracts with their own F&B providers.

- **Technology and Software**

  - Registration and lead retrieval: Customize your electronic registration process and enable exhibitors to leverage lead-management solutions to prove event return on investment (ROI).

  - Chatbots: Engage and inform attendees with user-friendly chat functions deployed before, during, and after the event, including fully integrated multichannel and voice-powered solutions.

  - Data integration software: Understanding what the data is telling you requires a pre-built event-tech-integration platform designed to reveal attendee insights and drive personalization.

  - Exhibit floor planning software: Streamlining show floor management to view and edit booth space and status in real time, helping manage inventory and increase revenue. Potentially useful to gain fire marshal approval.

- Analytics visualization: Centralized analytics software featuring a dashboard of key data points showing you what you need to know, when you need it.

- Sponsorship management portal: Virtual tours of your venue, real-time information on availability, and in-platform digital payment processing to help drive sponsorship sales.

- Virtual events platforms: Providing seamless technology interface, audience interaction, networking opportunities, and sponsorship options.

- Speaker content management software: Organizing event content and speakers' presentation materials.

- Polling and session engagement: Leveraging attendees' own devices to deploy second-screen engagement strategies during keynotes, learning sessions, meetings, and other interactions, including surveys, up-down voting, games, and more.

- Exhibits and Environments

  - Easy exhibit ordering: One online source to order everything for an exhibit, including turnkey services to have it delivered to the venue and loaded into the designated show floor location.

  - Custom design and fabrication: One-of-a-kind, professionally designed and built displays, booths, and exhibits.

  - Custom rentals: An eco-friendly solution that's also cost-effective.

  - Exhibit program management: Contracting with a team of professionals to streamline and supervise exhibit programs, from storage, transportation, and delivery and setup to packing up and moving on to another location or back to storage.

- Hybrid exhibits: Leveraging the latest AV and event technology solutions can help exhibitors bring powerful ideas to life while leveraging digital to reach new audiences.

- Mobile tours: Management of all aspects of touring properties, from venue selection and event contracts to attendee registration and lead management.

- Modular rental exhibits: Rental exhibits can be outfitted with custom graphics and reconfigured to fill almost any size space and optimize every opportunity while leveraging investments.

- Permanent installations: Agencies can help design, build, install, and maintain a permanent installation as part of a strategy that extends the brand and builds community.

- **Production and Audiovisual**

  - Studio broadcasting and live streaming: Virtual or hybrid events, new product launches, video press releases—most events benefit from studio broadcast professionals trained to activate brand-messaging platforms.

  - Keynote and breakout production: Coordination of all script development, editing, and visualization, including scenic, audio, and visual support; may include talent sourcing and management.

- Audiovisual design and production: Professional AV support, with the latest software and equipment to optimize lighting and sound design, engineering, and on-site execution. (Make sure they understand and honor American Society of Composers, Authors, and Publishers [ASCAP] licensing rules regarding music usage.)

- Digital displays and signage: Digital displays provide real-time schedules, improve venue navigation and interaction with content, and communicate changes and updates in real time consistently across the event campus.

- Projection mapping: Using technology to turn any surface (exteriors of buildings and interior ceilings, floors, and walls) into a video screen.

- Set, scenery, and special events design: Theater professionals use props, scenery, costumes, and technology as part of their scenic design solutions.

PRO TIPS:

- Establish a clear line of communication with all service providers. Regular check-ins can help ensure that everyone is on the same page and address changes or challenges promptly.

- If possible, organize site visits with relevant vendors.

- Prepare for unforeseen circumstances by developing contingency plans. Whether it's inclement weather or a vendor cancellation, having alternatives in place can help mitigate risks.

- Formulate a plan to gather feedback on the services provided as the event unfolds in order to review the overall success of the event and the performance of each service provider. Determine how this will be documented as part of the debrief phase to inform future planning.

CHAPTER 7

Build Sponsorships

TO-DO LIST:

- Think about sponsorship as a strategy. Sponsors can bring huge value to an event and take it to a higher level.

- Demonstrate how the opportunities you offer can help a potential sponsor and their intended audience.

- Use an aggressive sponsorship team who works with a broad range of clients, so they can connect you with potential sponsors they've worked with previously.

- Have the sponsorship team and talent acquisition experts combine their strengths to secure audience-relevant talent and boost audience acquisition.

Sponsorships must be given strategic consideration like every other marketing channel. View potential sponsors as another audience for your event. What do they want to get out of the partnership? How can you make your offering competitive with other channels vying for their marketing dollars?

Live events offer marketers something no other channel can touch: quality time spent with their target audience. Brands are working to offer deeper, more memorable connections, and marketers are taking a thoughtful, focused approach to their event strategy. Consider offering some exclusive aspect of your event (VIP lounge, exclusive meet and greet, private tour, etc.) as a turnkey sponsorship opportunity. This arrangement saves the sponsor costs and associates their brand with something their audience appreciates and values, integrating their brand into the event narrative.

If you demonstrate the value of your own year-round communications, you may be able to integrate sponsor brands and link their marketing message with your own.

TIME AND BRAND EXPERIENCE

When you're selling floor exhibits, remember that you're selling time, not space. The floor space has a fixed value, but time is contextual, with its value depending on what happens during the day. Time is our most valuable commodity.

Attendees invest time in your event by being there to take part. When your plan helps attendees find information, connects the right people, and rewards efforts with unique experiences, attendees will feel they got their money's worth for the time they invested.

Empathize with your audience personas and imagine how their needs change over time. Their energy levels wax and wane. Their sense of urgency fluctuates depending on how they feel and what happens next. People want spaces to chat, collaborate, rest their feet, or share what they've seen on social media. Activity in each space changes over time; how will you keep the experience fresh, unexpected, and inspiring?

If your event design includes a premium space, don't sell the space, which can only be sold once—sell time spent in that space. When you design space to showcase an ever-changing series of experiences and find sponsors for those experiences, you can generate new revenue and create an audience magnet on the trade show floor. Sponsorship becomes a tool to fund the design of time.

Sponsorship also helps prove a concept's value. If an idea doesn't earn sponsors, it may not add value. A sponsor requires quality time with their audience to establish a relationship. Time is the currency of brand experience. It's your job to make each experience count and to eliminate anything in your plan that wastes time. Time-sucks often take the form of legacy exhibits, agenda items, or ceremonies that still exist only because no one has chosen to reevaluate them.

Design brand experiences that make the most of the participants' time. Time that's been invested by attendees, exhibitors, sponsors, and hosts is the ROI that matters most. Design your event plan accordingly, and they'll be clamoring to return next year.

REFRESHING A SPONSORSHIP PROGRAM

When reassessing your sponsorship program, make sure it represents your organization in the best light. Sponsors want to be associated with like-minded professionals who reflect their brand and can deliver on marketing needs. Before launching a new sponsorship program, have your act together.

- Make sure the data you use to sell sponsorship packages is clean. Use data analysis to identify subsegments within your audience that might hold niche appeal to potential sponsor organizations. Use your analytical resources to demonstrate real marketing value to prospective sponsors.

- Understand how the wants and needs of audience personas align with your own event goals, then create opportunities (in-person, virtual, hybrid) to connect sponsors and attendee groups in meaningful, personalized ways. Integrated, custom sponsorships are attractive because they're authentic and add true value to the experience.

- Set up metrics for audience engagement, whether that's qualified lead generation or shifts in brand awareness or favorable impressions.

- Implement a plan to demonstrate the value you're selling sponsors, and back it up with on-site event staff trained to support sponsors and anticipate their needs.

- Update your year-round communication plan and identify opportunities to bring sponsorship messaging into your other channels.

If you've addressed these considerations, you're ready to refresh your sponsorship program and bring meaningful value to all.

SPONSORSHIP CHECKLIST

Consider these tips when developing a sponsorship program to bring added value to all stakeholders.

- **Play matchmaker.** Become a matchmaker between attendees and sponsors. Event sponsors prefer quality over quantity.

- **Strategize digital experiences.** Devote time, strategy, and tech tools to your virtual and hybrid sponsorship opportunities.

- **Make metrics matter.** Get your data house in order. To create personalized sponsorship offerings, accurately demonstrate ROI to your sponsors, and improve your strategy every year; you will need to show that you're effectively delivering value. Employ the right team and the right systems to collect and make sense of the data.

- **Know your strengths.** Be aware of other events your audience might attend and be clear about your unique advantages and audience acquisition strategy.

- **Align solutions.** Map sponsorship opportunities to the attendee journey. Align each audience persona's needs with event KPIs to determine the best solutions.

- **Know your sponsors.** Be aware of any exclusivity arrangements, contractual limitations, exhibitor conflicts, or any other potential problem, and address them well in advance of the event. Make sure your event support team understands these arrangements.

- **Cultivate community.** Find ways to create a community alongside your high-value sponsor partners, and take steps to keep it going year-round.

- **Think outside the event.** Work with sponsors to reduce waste and offer fewer, more meaningful, items. Partners may get better value from sponsoring a pre-event golf tournament, dinner, or other fun activity where engagement happens organically, beyond the parameters of the event venue.

- **Keep track of it all.** After the show, deliver a customized report to your sponsors. Record all promotional emails, social posts, pictures of their booth on-site, data and metrics, press mentions, testimonial quotes, etc., so that you can quickly and accurately follow up with sponsors after the event.

PRO TIPS:

- Think about your sponsorship goals. If there is a specific brand or sponsor category you want to attract that hasn't been part of your event, create a customized sponsorship plan for them, leveraging your year-round communication plan, and proactively meet with them to discuss it.

- Use data analytics tools to gather detailed insights about your event's audience, including demographics, interests, and engagement patterns. Create tailored sponsorship pitches that demonstrate how a sponsor's target audience aligns with your event attendees. Highlight specific data points that show potential ROI for sponsors, such as conversion rates from previous events or detailed attendee engagement metrics, showcasing your understanding of your event and the sponsor's business objectives.

- Instead of offering a one-size-fits-all sponsorship package, develop a tiered system that allows for customization and flexibility. Each level should offer increasing visibility and engagement opportunities but also include options for sponsors to tailor these benefits to better align with their goals. For instance, allow sponsors to choose between digital advertising, speaking opportunities, or exclusive branding of event segments. This flexibility can be especially appealing to sponsors with specific marketing strategies or target outcomes.

- Develop a comprehensive cross-promotion strategy that benefits both your event and your sponsors (co-branded content, joint social media campaigns, shared access to mailing lists, etc.), and leverage post-event content that highlights sponsor contributions, such as event recap videos or impact reports. Show potential sponsors the value of ongoing engagement with your audience to build enduring partnerships.

- Make a plan to nurture lower-tier sponsors; gracious support at this level can help build a pipeline of major sponsors for the future.

CHAPTER 8

Virtual Event Software

TO-DO LIST:

- **Choose the right platform to host your event:** Think about everything you want to accomplish with your virtual event—branding, interaction, training, entertainment—and select one platform that optimizes your plan.

- **Leverage data analytics for personalization:** Utilize advanced data analytics tools to analyze attendee behavior and preferences during your events. This involves tracking which sessions have the highest attendance, engagement rates in live polls, and Q&A sessions. Use this data to personalize the attendee experience in real time and for future event planning. For example, dynamically suggest sessions to attendees based on their engagement history or create personalized follow-up content that resonates with their interests.

- **Invest in robust cybersecurity measures:** With the increase in virtual events, cybersecurity is more critical than ever. Ensure that you're investing in high-quality, secure platforms and tools to protect your event from unauthorized access, data breaches, and other cyber threats. Consider conducting regular security audits, employing end-to-end encryption for communications, and training your team on cybersecurity best practices. Educate your attendees on how to protect their information and what measures are in place to safeguard their data.

continued

- **Offer hybrid event options for greater reach:** As you plan virtual events, consider the potential for hybrid models that combine both live and virtual elements. This approach not only accommodates attendees who can't travel due to restrictions or concerns but also expands your event's reach to a global audience. Implementing a hybrid model requires careful planning around technology integration, content delivery, and engagement strategies to ensure a cohesive experience for all participants.

VIRTUAL OPTIONS FOR LIVE, IN-PERSON EVENTS

Extending an event virtually exponentially increases reach and potential revenue. This allows you to connect with interested audiences around the world who are unable to physically attend your event while enabling people to easily sample your brand and engage incrementally. Virtual attendance opens up powerful new avenues for sponsorship opportunities, social sharing, and online communities. Virtual audiences have their own preferences and expectations, and smart marketers will leverage digital media according to their unique personas. Set yourself up for success: Start off by using the appropriate digital tools and producing quality content.

UNDERSTAND YOUR OPTIONS REGARDING BROADCASTING AND EVENT SOFTWARE

Choosing the platform to host your virtual event depends on what best suits your content and your audience. As you navigate options, be sure to differentiate between broadcasting and virtual event software.

Broadcasting distributes your video to your audience; it's the pipeline carrying video content to your attendees. The word *broadcast*, derived from the agrarian process of scattering seeds for new plants, is traditionally associated with transmitting programs via television or radio. In the events arena, the term refers to video hosting, video conferencing, webcasting, or digital streaming via such tools as YouTube, Vimeo, Facebook Live, Instagram Live, or LinkedIn Live.

Digital broadcasting can be designed to allow your audience to interact with your video content while they view it, whether live, prerecorded, or on-demand. For example, if you're planning a company announcement and want an easy, engaging way to share the information with employees, record the content and broadcast it, leveraging tools to optimize the audience experience.

USE STORYBOARDING TO CAPTURE TEMPORAL EVENT FLOW

Storyboarding helps you communicate the strategy behind your choices and helps decision-makers understand the user experience before it's created. Even the roughest of illustrations—a photo board or brief, clear descriptions of what's happening at each touch point across the span of time spent at the event—helps you lay things out in a visual sequence.

Present each moment of the journey using ideas, images, and possibly animation. Punctuate the story with exciting spectacles, calm reflections, and a range of interactions that demonstrate the actual cadence you want event attendees to experience. Make sure your core concept and planned execution are understood and can be stress-tested from multiple perspectives.

WHAT IS VIRTUAL EVENT SOFTWARE?

Virtual event software and digital event platforms are the ways your audience will access, engage, and interact with your content. Compare it to a meeting room, convention center, or hotel ballroom for your virtual event. These platforms are also often used for small meetings and webinars as well. Depending on your use case, you may sometimes use meeting software in conjunction with virtual broadcasting tools. If you require complex registration information, a virtual exhibitor hall, chat rooms, or multiple session tracks, consider a robust virtual event platform.

Most virtual event platforms include customizable home pages designed to match the look and feel of your brand or organization, with branded images, areas for featuring written and video content, and navigation to event information, registration, chat, and more. Virtual event software often embeds digital broadcasting video players like YouTube or Vimeo on pages that feature keynotes and sessions.

CHARACTERISTICS OF A GOOD VIRTUAL EVENT PLATFORM

- **Is simple** for your audience to access and navigate. User experience is key.

- **Enables customization** of colors, fonts, and images, so the virtual event is an extension of your organization or brand. Ideas for best practices, troubleshooting, and support should be offered.

- **Allows you to design the experience** of your virtual event, not just the look and feel of your event. If you plan to offer a virtual trade show, select an event platform with proven capability.

- **Offers engagement features** like chat and Q&A, so your audience can easily interact with speakers, exhibitors, and peers.

- **Provides multiple sponsorship opportunities** throughout, to increase revenue through your event.

- **Works seamlessly on all browsers and mobile platforms**, so attendees don't have to download any special software to participate.

- **Gives your team detailed reporting** so you can quantify value (and share key insights with sponsors). Ideally, real-time reporting shows you how many attendees are on-site and where, along with responsive solutions to issues.

- **Integrates with your existing event solutions** to cut down on manual work leading up to your event, like importing audience data.

- **Doesn't require a long-term contract.** Negotiate a deal that motivates everyone to achieve a great experience.

- **Makes sure it's a good experience** for your audience.

To better understand how digital broadcasting and event software relate to your virtual event, ask yourself how you want your audience members to interact with content, presenters, and each other. What will provide the best experience and create the most value for everyone?

Only you can determine the level of interaction you need to maximize the effectiveness of your content during and after your event. If you plan to generate press and social media shares, make it easy for your audience to engage.

Amp up engagement at your virtual event with tools like chat, comments, and the ability to like or react to content, transforming the audience from viewers to active participants. If you want to create a two-way dialogue between your audience and content creators, consider adding surveys, polling during live sessions, or allowing audience members to speak up during smaller breakout sessions.

BROADCAST TIPS

Internet connectivity can be your biggest potential obstacle to smooth streaming. Make sure your broadcast connection is wired ethernet (not wireless) and dedicated (not shared with other users). You don't want to encounter technical hiccups just because someone in another room is downloading a large file.

Use multiple high-definition cameras for wide shots, close-up shots, and audience footage. Place cameras on risers so they're eye level with the speakers and set the stage high enough to keep audience heads out of camera shots. For the best look, make sure the stage has a backdrop.

Meeting rooms are often dark, so proper lighting is crucial for broadcasting. Point directional lighting at the presenter from right and left, with smaller lights angled down toward the speaker's back shoulders for backlight. Wireless microphones eliminate snaking cords and look better on screen. An audio engineer can manage lapel mic placement, ambient noise, and other issues that might arise. Work with experienced pros, who will preempt most of the problems encountered by DIYers and first timers.

Rehearse, rehearse, rehearse. Step through everything with your tech crew before rehearsing with each presenter. Work out the bugs and then ensure that what they experience in rehearsal is consistent on show day. Unless you're working with professional presenters, consider offering presenter training. Speaking to a video camera is different from addressing a live audience; inexperienced presenters can come off as inauthentic.

REGISTRATION STRATEGY: VIRTUAL OR IN-PERSON

As you think about who you want to attend your event, remember that your registration plan is key to this part of your marketing strategy. (Who cares if it's the most innovative, exhilarating event on the planet if no one comes?) Every event and audience persona will have different needs. Design things so you're learning from each registrant to better meet their needs, fulfilling commitments to exhibitors and sponsors, and amplifying your audience acquisition strategy.

Scrutinize the on-site registration experience. For most attendees, their first live touch point with your event will be at the registration desk. Thanks to digitalization, many aspects of registration are much simpler than in years past, with an expedited process for speedy, efficient check-ins now the norm. Some events offer satellite registration at hotels supporting the event. Others offer kiosks, on-demand badge printing, and phone apps. You can downsize your on-site registration desk requirements while offering better service, a secure payment platform, and robust data analysis and reporting.

Learn about your attendees. People attending an event usually arrive with a goal in mind. Help them reach it by understanding their needs. Some items to request as they register may include—

- Basic information regarding their age bracket, job role, and personal interests

- Diversity, equity, and inclusion metrics

- Professional challenges and what success looks like to them

- How and where they access new information and on which topics

- Why they're interested in your event and what might prevent them from showing up

- Who they'd love to hear speak, perform, conduct a demo, etc.

- What they wish you could do differently

Always tell audiences why you're asking for this information: to make their event experience more relevant. You may use the information they give you to suggest a possible learning track that's ideal for them, meetups with like-minded attendees, exhibits of special interest, and after-the-event access to proprietary information, research, or white papers. Make it easy for your audience to give you the requisite permissions for any privileged information.

Be respectful:

- Don't ask questions if you aren't going to use the data.
- Limit the number of questions you ask.
- Don't use data without their permission.
- Always respect their privacy and treat their data with top digital security measures.

After people register, reinforce their decision by telling them exactly what to expect, including sponsors, exhibitors, presenters, and other relevant information. Based on what you learned from their registration profile, you could suggest extending their trip to enjoy exclusive leisure activities. Help them take advantage of your connections with the host city by offering resources they couldn't access on their own.

Utilize advanced engagement tools for networking: Networking is a key component of live events, which can be challenging to replicate virtually. Explore advanced virtual event platforms that offer innovative networking features that can help recreate the spontaneous connections that occur at in-person events and foster meaningful professional relationships.

- **AI-powered matchmaking:** Implement AI-driven algorithms to match attendees based on their interests, industry, job roles, and goals for attending the event. This technology can suggest potential connections and facilitate introductions, making networking more efficient and targeted.

- **Speed networking sessions:** Organize timed, one-on-one video networking sessions, mimicking the speed dating format. This format allows participants to meet a large number of attendees in a short amount of time, maximizing networking opportunities.

- **Gamification and incentives:** Integrate gamification elements to encourage networking, such as points, badges, or rewards for connecting with others, attending networking sessions, or participating in discussions. This can add a fun, competitive edge to the event.

- **Networking lounges:** Create virtual "lounges" or common areas where attendees can join impromptu video chats or group discussions. These spaces can simulate the informal networking that happens in physical event spaces.

- **Event mobile app:** Utilize a mobile app designed for the event that includes networking features. An app can facilitate easier connection building, schedule sharing, direct messaging, and even location-based networking suggestions for hybrid events.

PRO TIPS:

- **Enhanced AI-powered matchmaking:** Upgrade the AI matchmaking algorithm to analyze not just the attendees' profiles but also their engagement levels during the event. This includes session attendance, interaction in Q&As, and topics of interest expressed through chats and polls. The goal is to create hyper-personalized networking recommendations that evolve in real time, ensuring more meaningful and relevant connections.

- **Virtual reality (VR) networking spaces.** Transform virtual breakout rooms by leveraging VR technology, creating immersive networking environments that mimic real-world settings like conference halls, coffee shops, or thematic rooms related to the event's focus. Attendees can navigate these spaces using VR headsets or web interfaces, engaging in conversations through avatars. This approach adds a tangible sense of presence and can significantly boost engagement and interaction among participants.

- **Blockchain-enabled networking:** Utilize blockchain technology to create a secure and transparent networking environment. Implement digital passports for attendees, recording their participation, contributions, and connections made during the event. This not only enhances security and trust but also allows participants to carry their event credentials and networks to future events, facilitating long-term professional relationships.

- **Intelligent networking bots:** Deploy AI-driven chatbots that serve as networking facilitators, guiding attendees through the networking process. These bots can suggest topics of conversation, remind users of upcoming networking opportunities, and even initiate introductions between attendees with similar interests. By providing a more guided networking experience, attendees can navigate large virtual events more effectively.

- **Holographic presentations and networking:** Introduce holographic technology to deliver presentations and enable networking in a more interactive and engaging manner. Speakers, panelists, and attendees can be projected as holograms, offering a near-physical event experience. This technology can be particularly effective in hybrid events, allowing virtual attendees to feel more connected to the in-person aspect of the event and vice versa.

CHAPTER 9

Finalizing the Event Plan

TO-DO LIST:

- Scrutinize the event plan by giving it a thorough reality check. Seek input from the experts building or executing the plan.

- Ensure that health, safety, and risk-mitigation considerations are integral to the plan.

- Prototype and/or test concepts—especially those that are new or untried.

- Take a moment to make sure the design for each element is optimized for the space.

- Ensure that the planned graphics, signage, etc., are properly specced and will work as intended.

- Confirm the planned timing of each segment, ensuring there are buffer times for transitions.

- Confirm that you have the staff and budget to execute your event plan. (Even the best people can't be in two places at once.)

- While you are still finalizing the plan, pause to think further down the road—is there anything you will regret *not doing*? (For example, videotaping live sessions, hiring a photographer, inviting the press, etc.)

The critical finalization of an event plan bridges the gap between meticulous planning and flawless execution. Make sure your event plan is a ready-to-implement strategy for success, not just a blueprint.

MAKE SURE YOU'VE CHOSEN THE BEST POSSIBLE CONCEPT

Find people who can give your ideas a reality check—reviewing important considerations and key constraints (time, budget, and cost). If they have reservations, explore other ways to accomplish things. Consider whether a different approach can achieve the same goals while saving time or money. Take useful feedback into account and revise your concept accordingly. Here are a few ways to help ensure your event plan is feasible and optimized for success.

- **Engage expert reviewers for reality checks.** Seek feedback from experienced professionals, industry insiders, or trusted advisors. Choose individuals who have a keen eye for detail and can provide constructive criticism. Their insights can help identify potential pitfalls or areas for improvement that you might have overlooked.

- **Explore alternative approaches.** If feedback suggests that a particular aspect of your event might not be feasible, be open to exploring alternative methods. Sometimes, a different approach can achieve the same objectives more efficiently or in a more cost-effective way. This could mean adjusting the scale of your event, opting for a different venue, or rethinking your promotional strategy.

- **Prioritize cost-effective solutions.** While striving for the best, also seek out cost-effective solutions that do not diminish the value or impact of your event. This shift could involve negotiating with vendors, leveraging technology for efficiency, or finding creative ways to do more with less.

- **Incorporate valuable feedback.** Take feedback seriously when it comes from individuals with experience or expertise in event planning. Use this feedback to refine your concepts, ensuring they're still ambitious but grounded in reality.

- **Revisit and revise regularly.** Event planning is an iterative process. As you incorporate feedback and explore alternatives, revisit your plan regularly to ensure it remains aligned with your objectives, constraints, and the latest insights. This will help you stay on track and adapt to any changes or new opportunities that arise.

- **Focus on achieving your core objectives.** Throughout the planning process, keep your core objectives in focus. Every decision should contribute to achieving these goals, whether it's enhancing attendee experience, ensuring smooth logistics, or meeting financial targets.

- **Make sure safety protocols are in place as an integral part of the event plan.** Before the show begins to load into the venue, everyone should be trained on safety precautions and crisis-mitigation procedures.

- **Prepare for contingencies.** Plan for the unexpected. Identify potential risks and develop contingency plans for critical aspects of your event. This initiative-taking approach ensures you're prepared to handle challenges efficiently, minimizing disruptions to your event.

By following these steps, you can refine your event plan to ensure it's not only visionary but also practical, achievable, and aligned with your goals. The key is to balance creativity with pragmatism, leveraging feedback and expertise to create an event that is memorable, impactful, and seamlessly executed.

SHOW SITE RISK-MANAGEMENT GUIDELINES

The safety of all involved in event production needs to be a top priority—for everyone. The load-in and load-out of a show, involving forklifts, rigging equipment, carpet installation, etc., demands that everyone remain vigilant.

Each venue and location will have its own safety standards and compliance requirements. Each event will pose unique risks that must be evaluated, with specific mitigation and contingency plans in place well before the load-in date. (For example, shows that involve demonstrations of heavy machinery or are staged outdoors in potentially extreme weather will need to address those specific concerns.) Safety arrangements and emergency response procedures should be part of the event plan. In addition, they should be reviewed with the entire show team and shared as part of the "Know Before You Go" communications.

That said, the most effective deterrent to health and safety hazards is nurturing a safety-conscious culture. Fostering a safety-first mindset and articulating response plans well in advance of the event means that the show crew is prepared to jump into action if an incident occurs.

Ideally, dedicated safety/security professionals are represented on the team planning the event and attending on-site. Many corporations will have their own risk-management/security people on-site at events, and it's important to ensure that everyone is operating from the same playbook. Ultimately, the team handling general services should publish a Show Site Crisis Management Plan that addresses potential threats and hazards that could affect employees, customers, partners, operations, and any participants.

MANAGEMENT AND RISK MITIGATION
BEST PRACTICES

While there is no one-size-fits-all solution for optimizing safety and security at an event, the following list of best practices can help you start formulating your own show site risk-management guidelines.

- Make sure that the general services contractor has established risk management guidelines and related safety and health regulations that comply with Occupational Safety and Health Administration (OSHA) regulations and are part of standard operating procedure on show site.

- Prepare a crisis-management plan specific to the event that addresses "What to Do When" scenarios and includes contact information for all relevant parties. Include the show-site safety plan, venue protocols, emergency evacuation plans, etc., and distribute this to all event crew and team members prior to load-in.

- Make sure safety protocols are included in exhibitor kits.

- Promote a "Safety First" culture. Empower all show-site personnel to prevent accidents and injuries by exercising good judgment. Encourage them to refuse to do anything they consider unsafe, prevent/stop anyone from doing something unsafe, and listen to anyone reporting safety concerns.

- Identify an on-site safety coordinator. If this isn't possible, make sure someone in a supervisory role assumes this responsibility. Make sure everyone knows who to contact if they have a concern or witness an incident.

- Hold a safety meeting on-site to review these plans, address any concerns, and identify places in the venue to take shelter and/or regroup in case of an emergency. Include any security concerns, badge/ID protocols, or other information that could help keep your team safe.

continued

- Make sure everyone understands that only qualified professionals are authorized to work with or near electrical hazards, operate power equipment, engage with rigging equipment, etc.

- Practice fire safety. Enforce no-smoking policies; ensure combustible items are handled and stored safely. Work with the fire marshal to keep everyone safe.

- Once the event is underway, ask team leads to conduct regular walk-throughs and inspections to preempt any hazards that might develop.

- Keep "Safety Concerns" on the agenda for daily on-site production meetings, and use this time to review timely issues such as extreme weather, special staging events, wellness concerns, etc.

- Be prepared for medical emergencies. Have first aid supplies on hand, and make sure key people know where to find them. If emergency responders are not on-site, be clear about the appropriate response plan.

- Make sure all event staff are familiar with wellness protocols and can direct/assist attendees as needed during the event.

PROTOTYPE SOLUTIONS AND TEST THEM AS NECESSARY

Walk through the plan with the team and confirm that it still accomplishes what you've all set out to do. Make sure the concept is still achievable. Keep thinking about how to make it better. Continuously validate the plan with your team and outside subject matter experts (SMEs). Ask members of the original Renaissance team if you need to. Don't lock in the plan before it's ready. Always rethink the best way forward. You may find that some small detail added to one part of the plan totally disrupts something elsewhere; see if you can find a way to have each elevate the other.

Don't get so close to the plan that you miss obvious flaws. That's why it's important to find the right people to reality check each aspect of your plan. If experts say, "No way," don't argue. Instead, ask them to recommend other, better ways to approach the concept and make it achievable. Bring them into the process.

PROTOTYPE KEY CONCEPTS

Even in the age of CAD software, theatrical set designers typically build a tiny (1:24) 3D scale model of their set design to understand how it works from both a build perspective and in terms of audience sight lines. This practice helps solve issues and prevent problems, just for the price of card stock. Prototyping sounds complex, but it can be as simple or as elaborate as the concept merits. It's possible that a detailed storyboard does the job, but some concepts will need to be rendered as dimensional properties in order to be fully understood. It's also common practice to create a virtual fly-through of a theoretical event to demonstrate the attendee experience. Special effects, pyrotechnics, elaborate product reveals, or any kind of physical stunt should be created and rehearsed in a safe place before you commit to using them in front of a live audience.

Make sure the entire team has a chance to walk through the plan using the prototype. Challenge the team to ask questions and evaluate each milestone in the audience journey. Does the walk-through optimize flow and orchestration between discrete parts of the event? Does any area or exhibit fall short? Are there any pinch points in traffic flow? How can you make it better?

RAISE THE BAR WITH BEAUTY

When a specific item is created to support an event—a scenic element, booth, banner, etc.—the designer's intent is usually to help this piece contribute to the overall aesthetic while competing for attention on its own merits. A sign pointing to the restrooms or café may not need the same emphasis as the welcome banner, but even the humblest sign has a job to do, and the designer will help it do that by competing with beauty—that is, by using all of the design tricks available.

The creation of live experiences is naturally a collaborative event, but frustrations can arise when those asked for input on a design don't have the right skill sets or design vocabulary to convey their wishes. They may feel something is lacking but don't know what it is. (A standard joke among designers is that they often receive feedback like "make the logo bigger.") To help everyone contribute in the most useful way possible, try sharing and referencing a common design language. Here's a basic lexicon of ten classic design elements you can start with.

- **Color:** Connects to the emotional brain in a powerful, nonlinear, unspoken language.

- **Contrast:** The mechanism of clarity. The way our eyes establish the difference between the figure and the background, and the relationship of content to what's around it.

- **Proportion:** The relation of one thing to another— context is everything. Proportion is the mathematics of formal design.

- **Shape:** Carries the many associations of shared experience. A simple arrow pointing up has meaning.

- **Material:** Tells a story about what we're made of. If a chair is made of wood or steel, we make judgments about its user.

- **Texture:** Adds dimension to surface. It's the interface between body and object in the sensory language of touch.

- **Typography:** Shapes what we see and how we see it— from a romantic script font to a bold block type.

- **Time:** Design unfolds in time. Even so-called static objects are experienced in time. (A book unfolds in the hands and mind of the reader, lighting shifts, etc.)

- **Image:** Figurative images and visual conventions telegraph content and evoke emotional connection.

- **Content:** Typographic expression stands as the foundation of meaning behind visual forms.

THE HANDOFF: TRANSLATING CREATIVE CONCEPTS INTO GRAPHICS AND 3D OBJECTS

You've already agreed on the approved graphic theme for the event, and you know how it looks on invitations, venue entrances, registration booths, custom exhibits, or whatever else you need for your event. Your design team has already provided a general template or style guide to help create each itemized deliverable.

It's now the graphic design team's job to add the actual content for each piece. Each wayfinding sign, each entrance, each banner placement requires its own high-resolution graphic file ready for printing. For a large exposition or trade show, this can be an exhaustive list of deliverables, including access to an online tool to list and track progress and approvals for each item. The approved deliverables list will have a line number for each item and an explanation of what it is and where it will be placed during the event. The list may note ceiling height and other restrictions as appropriate, along with a digital image file showing what each piece looks like. A detailer has already made sure the design works from an engineering perspective and has structural and performance integrity. (Does it need to withstand wind and weather? Does it accommodate any electronics that will be added? Will it do everything it needs to without collapsing or tipping over? etc.) Depending on the process in place, these approved files will include refined graphic files, blueprints, or detailed build plans.

At this point, as you prepare to build, each line item has already been produced in layout, showing the final look of each piece, created in the exact dimensions and resolution required for production. If there has been a change to a logo, a font, a sponsorship requirement, or similar universal edit—potentially affecting every deliverable—these details will have already been corrected on each individual file. A common error is to use a brand logo that's in the system from the previous event; logos are often changed, updated, or subject to new guidelines. From the start, ask for new brand graphics, and make sure the authorized people have signed off on their use. (That's why we emphasize rigorous approval processes early in the planning phase.) Ensure that each approved and finalized line item has also been attached to a graphic production order and scheduled to be printed or fabricated, then put into production.

For 3D elements, the process of review, validation of blueprint or build plans, and required approvals is similar, but build plans for exhibits and physical properties generally require review by a master carpenter or fabrication engineer. Since graphics are often applied to these pieces, there must be coordination between graphics and fabrication to ensure everyone is using the latest approved files.

The later in the process you make revisions, the more expensive it will be. Scrutinize design files early, share information, and make sure everyone has signed off on the build plans, so things will progress smoothly when it matters. Because the process of turning ideas into build plans involves making revisions, be sure to document and communicate every modification, even seemingly minor ones. Everyone on the team needs to stay aware of the interdependencies of the various disciplines responsible for delivering the plan. Be proactive about reaching out as soon as possible to any department heads whose assignments are affected, and collaborate on a solution that works best for everyone.

The process of documenting these adjustments can most likely be accommodated within the software your team is already using to track progress on each deliverable in the build plan; make sure you're able to track and review all changes made after the plan was approved. One change can affect others, and if the change brings cost savings in one area, you may be able to apply that elsewhere, keeping an eye on anything that affects budget reconciliation. For learning purposes, it's important that you understand what happened so that your team can avoid mistakes and embrace improvements the next time around.

Steadfastly monitor the project as it's being built; continue to track any tweaks or adjustments that need to be made during the process of building each part of the event; find out if there's a budget impact; and share the final outcome with the entire team.

Design exhibit materials for delivery excellence. As the team prepares to build prototypes, take the opportunity to assess each item. Are you using the best material for the job? Is a more sustainable version available? Every year brings new breakthroughs in materials, fabrication techniques, digital services, and AV technology.

Require close coordination and communication between the creative teams who imagined the concept and the operations people who execute. All aspects must be rigorously managed. An individual production designer or team of specialists will act as go-betweens who translate the creative vision into specific instructions for the fabricators, graphic printers, carpenters, AV technicians, and others on the build team. They have experience in creating experiences—they are the alchemists who turn the sketches, strategies, and iterative plans into gold. They maintain an open line of communication with both teams so that any questions can be raised, answered, and resolved in an expedited manner. Their job is to predict and prevent any disconnects. They understand what's required, whether the audience is a hundred high-powered executives or tens of thousands of people coursing through a three-million-square-foot campus.

FINALIZE THE EVENT PLAN

Progress on finalizing the event plan generally proceeds along two parallel and interdependent paths. While the agency's creative team works to define the event experience in vivid detail, the production team works to verify that everything can be delivered on time, within budget, and with the integrity of the essential concept intact.

Both teams need to scrutinize the event plan by asking tough questions: Do you have sufficient staff to execute the plan? Does everyone know their role? (The plan should clarify who is responsible for designing, building, installing, and managing the event on-site.) Does the plan make any assumptions that should be challenged? If there are multiple vendors working directly with the event manager, accountability can be dangerously vague. Clarify all roles, codependencies, and responsibilities, and itemize what is and is not included in each budgetary line item. This step can be especially challenging if the event manager or the agency team lack experience with some aspect of the event. Whenever a plan calls for something out of the ordinary, validate the plan with a subject matter expert.

- **We don't know what we don't know.** Ask probing questions and seek out experts who can review the plan for hidden costs. For example, if you're displaying something of great value and delicacy, your budget must include handlers and security staff to protect it. If your guest speaker is a government official or a former president, you'll be required to follow strict protocol and vacate certain areas of the venue. If guest presenters have any special equipment requirements, are you allowed to live stream their content or share it on the event website? Does your entertainment have an obscure rider in their contract that requires a cash outlay? Every choice has ancillary budget implications.

- **Expect the unexpected.** If you haven't already, review the event plan from the perspective of a pessimist. Ask what could possibly go wrong, and then consider evasive action and emergency plans accordingly. Natural disaster responses? Power outages? Traffic delays? Stormy weather at an outdoor event? Think about contingency options and how they affect your budget and space requirements. Will decibel limits or local ordinances regulate the hours your event can operate? These should be acknowledged in the proposal. Are there plans to travel and then restage some portion of the event at other venues? You'll need to make sure the exhibit materials and AV technology can be transported and installed with minimal fuss and expense.

- **Train the team.** Anticipate in your budget the time and expense required to communicate the plan to those who will make it happen. Some events use volunteers to staff special events or hospitality areas, who need to be trained, given uniforms, and supplied with all necessary materials. Have each lead person on the team sign off on the budget items they're responsible for delivering. If any items in the budget are left unsigned, make sure they find an owner, so they're covered.

GLIMPSE THE FUTURE

After the event—what comes next? Consider how to support aspects of the event through other channels, perhaps as part of a broader marketing plan. Maybe there's a digital component that runs yearlong, launched from the live event platform. Or maybe your plan includes a look at how the concept evolves in the coming years to attract a steady stream of earned media coverage.

PRO TIPS:

- Ensure every team member, vendor, and stakeholder has an updated and detailed timeline that includes all event aspects from setup to breakdown, with specific times and responsibilities.

- Leverage quiet time and white space. A nonstop stream of memorable moments, learning sessions, exhibits, market activations, and social events can also be counterproductive. If there are too many activities or too many demands being placed on event participants, it's hard to break through the noise.

- Collaborate with 3D artists to bring creative concepts to life through immersive installations and interactive displays, elevating the event to new heights of engagement and excitement.

- Develop a comprehensive waste management plan that includes measures for reducing, reusing, and recycling waste generated by the event.

- For outdoor events, have a solid plan B in case of inclement weather, including tents, indoor backup locations, and communications plans for notifying attendees of changes.

- If the event involves VIP guests, finalize the details for their arrival, seating, accommodation, and any special requests or security measures.

Once the Event Plan is approved, it's time to build it.
Jump to chapter 12 to start learning about
phase 3 or stick around for our special sections
for exhibitors in chapters 10 and 11.

CHAPTER 10

For Exhibitors: Leverage Every Opportunity

TO-DO LIST:

- Create a plan to make the most of your opportunity and gain the highest possible return on your investment by achieving your objectives.

- Be clear about who you want to attract to your exhibit and how you will engage with them and add value to their experience.

- Develop a marketing plan/activation strategy for connecting with prospects.

- Showcase your product or service to have the greatest impact on the people who matter most. Consider whether new technology can help tell your story.

- Begin planning as far ahead as possible; allow three months, at minimum.

- The GSC will publish an online exhibitor kit (or exhibitor manual) with all event information, rules, regulations, deadlines, and order forms. Rules vary by city and change over time, so always review the exhibitor kit.

Before you sign up to exhibit at an event, make sure it's right for your brand or business, will attract qualified leads, and helps fulfill your own objectives. Be specific about whether your own success metrics align with the event. If they line up nicely, get ready to leverage every opportunity this event offers.

Exhibiting at an event can be expensive and time consuming. Done right, however, it can also be rewarding in terms of brand experience, lead generation, and actual sales growth. A live experience that leverages personalized engagement is the ultimate brand experience. The majority of attendees say that engaging with branded event marketing experiences convinced them to purchase a product. Exhibitors must leverage the opportunity to maximize their investment.

RENTING VERSUS OWNING AN EXHIBIT

Businesses making their first foray into the world of trade show marketing have many decisions to make about their needs as exhibitors. It can be hard to predict how much room is needed to present your product, meet with prospects, stock merchandise, and sufficiently represent your brand. Rental booth exhibits offer almost endless options while letting you try out different approaches and configurations. You can learn what works best and deploy different tactics specific to each event. Rental systems are designed to let you switch up messaging and graphics from show to show, to test and learn what attracts the most qualified traffic. Refresh your branding to tailor it for each audience. If you only attend a couple of shows a year, the rental option may meet your needs. But if you have a full travel agenda, your own customizable display may be a worthwhile investment. Whether you need to replace a road-worn exhibit or are starting from scratch, your exhibit partner can find a solution that works for you.

DESIGN A BUSINESS PLAN

Build out your action plan, designate roles and responsibilities, and make sure everyone on your team is aware of the show's official partners, so they know who to reach out to if and when help is needed. The agency or GSC should have an exhibitor services team available to support everything, from designing your exhibit to getting it in and out of the venue on time.

Align your plan with your budget. Account for things like travel and lodging, event registration, exhibit space rental, booth design/activations, show services (carpet/flooring, furniture, audiovisual, electrical, lead retrieval, etc.), shipping and transportation of materials, marketing, giveaways, and any sponsorship fees. Do you need to create a custom graphic design, engage in special promotions, or feed those staffing your exhibit? Make sure you are familiar with the exhibitor kit published by the show organizer or GSC. Think through your costs and be prepared for miscellaneous needs that invariably arise.

Your business plan should include a strategy for marketing your presence at the event. You can get the word out through various marketing channels and publications, along with your own organization's website and social media. Give people a reason to seek you out, and make it easy for them to find you.

DESIGN AN ENGAGEMENT PLAN

At an event, you're competing for the attention of potential customers. If you don't capture their attention, someone else will. Make a plan to attract and engage with the most qualified attendees: those not just hunting for swag but actually in need of your products and services.

The method you use to engage with prospects depends on your goals. Will a riveting product demonstration encourage visitors to learn more? Does your product story require the use of technology, prototypes, or detailed graphics to make it easy to understand? Would you rather reach many people with a general impression of your offering, or secure a few consultative appointments?

TIERS OF ENGAGEMENT

Think about your engagement strategy as a series of steps.

- First, attract your audience with creativity that can be spotted across the show floor. Use shapes, colors, sounds, smell, and taste if you can.

- Then, hold your visitors with relevant messages that mean something to them and their challenges. Use conversation and tech elements like AR/VR to build engagement.

- Finally, close the transaction with genuine interaction.

1. **Be clear** about what you want to accomplish.

2. **Prioritize** the following goals or add your own to the list.

3. **Focus** your efforts and resources on achieving the top three.

   - Raise brand awareness.
   - Enhance brand perception.
   - Generate leads or grow your pipeline.
   - Launch new products.
   - Launch new initiatives.
   - Maintain key client relationships.
   - Make connections within your industry.
   - Recruit new employees.
   - Educate clients on new products and features.

If you're launching an entirely new product that has been speculated on in industry media, work the curiosity factor by creating a special demo/workshop area that teases the audience but doesn't reveal everything unless they step inside. For example, a space with translucent walls can let people sense images, actions, and movement inside but requires attendees to step inside for the full experience. Live video (fed to an outward-facing booth monitor and also to your website) can tempt casual viewers to discover more.

Think about ways your exhibit space can serve your key clients and build relationships. Sometimes offering people a place to sit down while they recharge their devices is sufficient motivation to network with you. Participate in the event's networking sessions and listen to what people are talking about, then use those insights to make your own pitch more relevant to their needs.

DESIGN A DIGITAL MARKETING PLAN

Digital marketing helps you leverage your investment inside and outside the show floor. By adopting proven digital marketing practices, you can reach your audience before, during, and after the show.

Before the event: Create buzz before the show using customized microsites and landing pages shared on social media. Give visitors exclusive offers or sneak peeks at products you'll be revealing on-site. Digital tools make it easy to access analytics; learn what you can before the show to polish your approach. Use email marketing tools (segmentation is key) and send relevant messages to the prospects and customers you expect to attend the show. Make it worth their while to spend time at your booth. If possible, schedule appointments ahead of time to offer meaningful consultations and add value for existing customers.

During the event: Continue to build momentum during the show. Walk the show floor to see what other exhibitors are doing. Keep your social media relevant, commenting on what's happening on-site or offering a play-by-play of key events. Arrange to meet up with people and cultivate dialogue and interaction among exhibitors, attendees, and guest speakers.

- **Lead generation is a priority:** Consider a real-time lead-tracking app or interface as part of your tech plan to manage your pipeline on the fly. Ask the team about CRM integration and the options they have to leverage registration data as part of your personalization strategy.

- **Data-driven personalization:** Data analysis opens the door to greater personalization. With participant permission, you can design customized experiences within larger events, streamline agendas for the individual, distill the narrative of their personal experience, help them cross paths with other people in synergistic ways, and even offer them esoteric and exclusive experiences. Companies seeking qualified leads help offset the monetary cost of an exhilarating, personal experience in exchange for the opportunity to offer that individual something they've already expressed an interest in.

- **After the event:** Extend connection after the show. Most of the visitors to your exhibit will remember their interactions with you months after the show. Social media channels relating to your event, industry, and affiliations will be tuned in to news about the show, so it's a great time to gain followers who will stay with you year-round. Follow up with personalized emails to loyal customers and new contacts; in advance, create a template of information you want to share, making it easy to respond in a timely manner. Update your website's content. Post photos or videos you took of interesting exhibits or presentations, share links to content you've created, offer giveaways, then tap into web analytics to see what gets the best results.

DESIGN A CHATBOT STRATEGY

According to a study by *Chatbot Magazine*, two out of three millennials in the US say they're likely to purchase products and services from brands using a chatbot.[1] Complement your staff by using a chatbot to answer your customers' most frequently asked questions. Free up your staff to perform as true consultants while providing an interactive way for people to sample your message. If they like the chatbot, they may hang around until your staff is free to personally assist them.

- **Solidify your strategy.** Put your chatbot to work for your brand.

  - Virtual assistants and chatbots can pull people into your booth, increasing engagement and valuable leads, and can also be part of the remote experience.

  - A smart digital partner with event expertise and coding capabilities can help you create a unique chatbot experience that you can control.

  - Design your bot and your booth simultaneously. Make sure the space lets your chatbot shine—in person and online.

  - If you're updating an existing booth, use the bot in a way that adds fun and useful interaction and complements a seamless presentation.

  - Use your bot as a source of data gathering and lead generation.

- **Make it fun.** A chatbot with a little attitude helps you create an experience that draws attendees to your booth. Gamify the experience with trivia questions, jokes, and funny stories that

---

1 ProProfs Editorial Team, "67% of Millennials in the US Reported That They Would Likely Purchase Products and Services from Brands with Chatbots," *Chatbots Magazine*, May 7, 2024, https://www.proprofschat.com/blog/chatbot-statistics/.

are relevant to the industry or association, or design the chatbot to serve as a virtual concierge that can guide attendees to a richer experience.

- **Build relationships.** Kick-start engagement by promoting your chatbot in your pre-event marketing and social media. Program your chatbot to send personalized emails or text follow-up messages in real time.

- **Test, test, test.** The last thing you want from your investment is a chatbot that's a frustrating experience for your audience. Before you launch, roll up your sleeves and try to break the chatbot (with unusual/devious requests). Check for technical jargon your audience is likely to use.

- **Build lots of fallbacks**—preprogrammed responses that help your chatbot handle questions that aren't included in its programming. If your bot has a custom content management system, you can make real-time changes on the fly, straight from the show floor, or online during virtual gatherings.

- Shop around to make sure you have a digital partner who knows what questions and answers to include, how to word them, and what's required to thoroughly test and secure quality assurance before go-live.

PRO TIPS:

- **Implement real-time sentiment analysis:** Equip your chatbot with real-time sentiment analysis capabilities, providing personalized responses and interventions. If there's a dip in engagement, the chatbot can offer incentives and fun facts, or prompt interactive sessions to reengage attendees.

- **Integrate augmented reality (AR) features:** Enhance the chatbot experience by integrating AR features into your platform, from guiding attendees through the event space to AR information overlays about speakers, exhibits, or products. Such features provide practical utility while building excitement and engagement, making your event more memorable.

- **Leverage advanced data analytics for post-event insights:** Coordinate with the event organizer to understand what composite data they can share to help all exhibitors plan future activations more strategically. Beyond immediate assistance and engagement, use the data collected by your chatbot for deep post-event analysis. Compare your data to information published by the event organizer. This includes attendee behavior patterns, most requested information, peak interaction times, and feedback on various aspects of the event. Leveraging machine learning algorithms can uncover insights to refine future event planning, personalize follow-up communications, and improve overall event strategy.

- **Ensure robust integration with event management platforms:** To maximize efficiency, your chatbot should seamlessly integrate with existing event management platforms and tools. This integration enables real-time updates to schedules, speaker lineups, and session changes, ensuring the chatbot provides accurate, up-to-date information. Additionally, integration with ticketing and CRM systems can facilitate personalized interactions, such as reminding attendees of their scheduled sessions or follow-ups on inquiries.

- **Prepare for scalability and unexpected demand:** Anticipate and prepare for spikes in chatbot interactions, especially during key moments of your event (e.g., during keynote speeches or right after session sign-ups go live). Optimize your chatbot's infrastructure for scalability, ensuring it can handle sudden increases in queries without degradation in performance. Consider implementing a Cloud-based solution with auto-scaling capabilities and stress testing your chatbot system ahead of the event to identify and rectify potential bottlenecks.

CHAPTER 11

For Exhibitors: Design Your Space

TO-DO LIST:

- **Optimize space utilization:** Plan your space efficiently to include interactive areas, product displays, and private meeting spots without feeling crowded.

- **Design for impact:** Create a visually appealing and attention-grabbing design that reflects your brand identity and stands out in a busy event environment.

- **Invest in high-quality graphics:** Ensure your visuals are of high quality and effectively communicate your brand message and value proposition.

- **Incorporate technology:** Utilize digital displays, interactive kiosks, strategic lighting, or augmented reality to make your booth engaging and memorable.

- **Display product:** Showcase your products in an accessible and attractive manner, allowing attendees to easily interact with them.

- **Refresh and update:** Regularly refresh your booth's design and messaging to reflect any new products, services, or brand updates.

continued

- **Add interactive elements:** Incorporate elements that encourage participation, such as live demos, interactive screens, or gamification features.

- **Train your team:** Ensure your staff is well trained, approachable, and knowledgeable about your products and services to enhance the overall experience for visitors.

- **Add networking areas:** Designate areas within your booth where meaningful conversations can take place away from the crowd.

- **Be accessible:** Make sure your booth is accessible to everyone, including those with disabilities.

- **Practice sustainability:** Incorporate eco-friendly practices and materials in your booth design and operations.

- **Get feedback:** Plan to collect feedback from visitors. After the event, analyze the performance of your exhibit against your objectives to measure success and identify areas for improvement.

Design a space that stands out while communicating your brand's message and your solutions for attendees' needs. Maximize your booth's potential to attract and engage your target audience. This chapter is a comprehensive guide to designing your exhibit space so it resonates with attendees and drives the results you want.

Before you decide on your physical exhibit design, imagine the experience you want to create. Keep budget parameters and goals in mind. Will you rent, build, or use some hybrid format that lets you insert customized panels or LED monitors into a reusable modular structure? If your exhibit will be used at multiple venues, consider a modular design that can be reconfigured for a variety of spaces. You don't need a huge or extravagant booth to catch attendee interest—you just need a booth that aligns with your objectives. Attendees are looking for solutions to their own business needs, and you want them to look your way. Use the opportunity of building a new booth to design an ideal space for the results you want. Your mission is to create an engagement experience people will be raving about after the show.

Hone your exhibit design. Work with the show's exhibitor services team or your own exhibit designer to create a booth that optimizes your specific opportunity as part of a larger ecosystem. (Sachel Josefson, a professor at Bemidji State University in Minnesota, reminds undergraduate designers that each exhibit is part of a celebration for that respective industry. Each design exists in the context of that community of practice.) Exhibit designers are only as good as their clients let them be. Tell the design team everything imaginable about your brand promise, graphic standards, customer experience, and vision for the future. Be sure to ask the show manager for attendee demographics to provide your design team in advance.

Here are some of the questions a thoughtful exhibit designer (and many other event services providers) may ask you:

- Who do you want to attract and why?

- Do you have experience or insights into how these people think, act, and behave?

- Do you need a space within your space for VIP handling?

- What do you hope trade show attendees get from the experience? Information, insight, inspiration?

- What do you need to accomplish? Lead generation, actual sales, brand building?

- What barriers might keep attendees away from your booth or your business? What will remove them?

- Do you have a compelling competitive story that needs to stand out?

- If you exhibited previously, what did you learn from that?
- If it's your brand's very first time exhibiting, what is your engagement plan?
- Do you have existing clients who will be at the show? Are they open to offering their insights or visiting you on-site to provide feedback?
- How will your booth be oriented? (Consider things specific to your assigned location on the show floor. Understand where you are in relation to the traffic flow and design your exhibit accordingly.)
- What is your location relative to your competitors, the show entrance, food service, and meeting space?
- Do you need to plan around structural aspects of the hall, such as columns, fire cabinets, cabling racks, and such?
- What can you expect regarding traffic flow in and out of the aisles that lead to your booth?
- What is the ideal booth height, given the ceiling restrictions? (Consider the side walls of the booth next to you. For example, if they have a high graphic wall, your plans for an open space won't work. Consult with the show management team to gain information that will help you make the best decisions.)
- What are the specific requirements of the products you want to display? Are they large, heavy, or unwieldy? Are there any safety concerns? Are there required permits?
- Do you plan to reuse the booth or repurpose any display assets?

Optimize your booth size and location. Today's booths incorporate learnings from the pandemic that accommodate health and safety protocols. In most US venues, baseline packages are predetermined for booths, so options for booth size and location will vary by show. Exhibitors usually have up to four options for booth location:

- In-line (positioned in a series with only one side open to the aisle)

- Perimeter (in-line, but set along a back wall so that higher booth heights may be allowed)

- Peninsula (located at the end of an aisle with three sides exposed to traffic

- Island (in the middle of the show floor, exposed to traffic on all four sides)

The experience, however, needn't be limited by booth boundaries; events often intermingle exhibit booths with networking and other experiences to feel more like a museum or retail experience. Design your booth for ultimate event flexibility. The most common and affordable option will usually be a standard in-line booth space, which uses a 10' x 10' or 10' x 20' footprint. Rental booths are a great option because they can be customized to fully represent a brand without requiring a long-term plan to maintain and store the property.

Design to arrest the senses. Talk to the designers creating your exhibit to understand the full range of graphic and AV tools available. Even a small booth can have a huge impact if the design of the exhibit grabs attention, and the content is intriguing. Keep in mind that the initial cost of designing and fabricating a knockout exhibit can be spread over multiple shows—the audiences will be different, but their interests will be similar.

What really matters is that the exhibit you create conveys an impression (and curates content) firmly tied to your business goals and your target audience's needs. Arresting images, AV techniques, and event technology can draw attendees into your exhibit and provide an eye-catching, engaging introduction to your brand. You want to motivate your customers, invite their confidence, and answer their questions.

Light it up. Do you have a vital message to share? Design elements literally shine a positive light on your unique products and services.

- Lighting can boost your competitive edge by creating contrast and drawing attention to key elements in your exhibit that others don't offer.

- Intelligent lighting—moving lights programmed to create a path with colors and designs—can help direct traffic and draw in prospects.

- Accent lighting can add a bit of flair to product showcases or even your logo.

- Softer, ambient lighting in consultation rooms can create a sense of refuge from the general show floor commotion.

- The use of "gobos"—lighting effects that project a logo or brand name onto the floor or other surfaces—are useful in places where a permanent graphic would feel intrusive.

- In the long term, strategically designed lighting elements used consistently in your booths from show to show can increase brand recognition.

Leverage content, graphics, and signage. Effective graphics draw attendees into your exhibit and provide an engaging introduction to your brand. The content you deliver needs to resonate with your audience and provide something they've been looking for, even just an answer. But just as important as what you say is how you say it. Designers consider the physical, philosophical, and psychological elements of the overall experience they want to create. Digital signage and interactive screens leverage eye-catching design with testimonial quotes, answers to frequently asked questions, new product developments, key features and benefits, and more via self-guided kiosk stations.

Benefits of digital displays:

- **Attractive:** Eye-catching and informative digital displays energize your space.

- **Interactive:** Encourage attendees to touch, play, and engage with your display. As a second-screen bonus, opt for virtual content that can also be streamed to visitors' mobile phones and remote attendees' screens.

- **Convenient:** Unlike printed signage that can be made obsolete, it's easy and instantaneous to revise digital text or swap out images on-site.

- **Immediate:** Real-time functionality enables content to be updated throughout the show based on what's happening in the moment.

- **Unique:** LED displays can convey motion and dimension in an otherwise flat space.

- **Flexible:** Build digital displays as standard video screen rectangles (either singly or into a wall of several screens), set them into creative elements like columns and totems, or intermingle them with printed graphics and product display areas.

- **Reinforce branding:** Designs can be customized to incorporate branding elements, such as color schemes, brand themes, or animated logos.

- **Engage while they wait:** Provide helpful information about products or services while attendees wait to speak with booth staff (useful during high traffic).

- **Demo the impossible:** Interactive digital displays enable you to showcase products that are too large, costly, or fragile to transport to the event.

BEST PRACTICES FOR BOOTH DESIGN:

- **Keep messages short, simple, and clear.** Scrap long paragraphs and lengthy lists of features and replace them with bold, captivating artwork. You have five seconds to grab attention, so make those seconds count. (Let your booth staff, handouts, and digital downloads be your information resources.)

- **Make it personal.** What's top of mind for your audience? How does your product or service answer their needs? Tap into emotional content with images that inspire and connect.

- **Signage should target the line of sight.** Present important images and messages at eye level. People read from top left to bottom right, so position your most important message on top to make sure it gets read. Use elegant, simple fonts. San serif is easiest to read; ALL CAPS is hard to read and feels like shouting.

- **Spur action.** Use messages that entice your visitors to do something—interact with your product, take a survey, or share an experience.

- **Pay attention to audio dynamics.** Make sure your digital displays hit home even without any sound, so noisy show floors or volume restrictions won't keep people from understanding your message. That said, ambient audio or directed sound can generate music and sound effects in a designated, defined area. An audio engineer can create a soundscape (rain, waves, wind) or pump up the energy level in a way that reinforces the brand. Perhaps you need to isolate part of your exhibit to create a soundproof consultation room or video theater. Talk to your exhibit designer, and they'll make it happen. (Make sure you have honored any ASCAP licensing requirements for music usage.)

Design a VR/AR strategy. Thanks to technology, you can make a 10' x 10' footprint feel as vast as outer space. Virtual reality (VR) and augmented reality (AR) technologies allow brands to create irresistible, immersive experiences that build lasting memories and positive brand associations. Digital immersion experiences engage audiences beyond actual users, generating show floor excitement and social media buzz. Because the technology behind immersive experiences is constantly improving, they're more attainable than you might think and easily scalable in scope, application, and budget. As part of your engagement strategy, AR/VR can be a smart way to:

- Improve and deepen attendees' experience with your brand, no matter how they engage, physically or virtually.

- Reinforce your brand and help you share important content easily.

- Cut through crowd noise and other distractions, allowing participants to focus on your message.

- Enhance virtual and hybrid events.

- Generate valuable data that can be used to refine in-person and digital strategies.

- Highlight features about your offering that may go overlooked or that may normally be impractical to bring to the show floor.

Leverage the power of immersive technologies to attract attendees, connect on a meaningful level, and elevate your brand. Spatial experiences can be a great option if your product is difficult to bring to the show floor or is still in production. Spatial reality (SR) uses a headset to interact with and explore the environment. These technologies are all good solutions for upleveling the virtual exhibit, enabling people across the globe to connect online in a world of your making. Using VR, you can combine video, 3D animation, and sound into an interactive AR experience that takes guests to the peak of Mount Everest, to swim to the ocean floor, or to journey inside the human brain. Immersive experiences create opportunities for fun photo ops that attendees will want to share on social media. Create a virtual playground for remote guests via chat platforms where they can interact in real time.

TELL YOUR BEST STORY

More events will be hosted in the Metaverse. Unless you're a technology developer, the smartest action you can take is learning about what's working and focusing on what you can control—your story. A good storyteller can take advantage of any platform available; for the near future, these will probably be variations and hybridizations of event and video game technology.

Regardless of your tech medium, start with your own authentic, relevant, irresistible, and inspirational story. Think about the kinds of images and video that would best connect your brand to the people you want to reach and work backward to the right technology solution. Make sure you're working with experienced providers who know how to incorporate health and safety protocols, lead-generation tools, and data analysis into the experience while fulfilling your immersive goals.

WISDOM FROM EXPERIENCED EXHIBITORS:

- **Be consistent.** Don't overhaul your brand identity for a specific show or event. Be sure that your booth design, materials, and messaging match what attendees will find if they visit your website.

- **Be direct.** Make sure the design of your booth, your messaging, and your materials clearly articulate what your company specializes in. You only have a few seconds to get your message across—so be simple and clear!

- **Be unique.** Stand out from the crowd! Don't be afraid to tap into some of the bolder colors in your branding. And definitely incorporate digital elements into your offerings. Anything that catches the eye and draws attendees in—as long as it's on-brand—is a win.

- **Look up.** Consider overhead signage to add some vertical interest to your booth. Just be aware that this will require tapping into rigging, a service provided by skilled laborers.

- **Look down.** Many show organizers provide carpet, but not all of them. Sometimes, supplying carpet for your booth is a requirement. That said, the use of floor decals is increasingly offered as a more environmentally friendly solution. Your exhibit fabricator can advise you in this regard. Also note that a raised floor may look nice but drives higher load-in costs.

- **Be prepared.** Think about what else you might need in your booth. Storage? A meeting space? A power supply? A robust internet connection? Take all of your requirements into consideration when working on your booth design.

DESIGN A BOOTH-STAFFING STRATEGY

- Build and train a diverse booth team that includes salespeople, along with other representatives from across the organization.

- Keep at least one SME on hand.

- Anticipate the questions visitors to your exhibit will have, and preplan demonstrations that answer them in a memorable way.

- Provide your booth associates with email templates they can use to immediately follow up with prospects who visit your booth.

- Rehearse and role-play with the booth team if your planned experience is nuanced or at all complex.

- Use your booth team to demonstrate to visitors what your brand cares about.

BEYOND THE BOOTH

Technology enables you to treat the exhibit or booth as a hub or headquarters for a full panorama of marketing outreach. You can offer livestreaming and/or on-demand video for attendees who prefer to attend virtually, allowing your content to be shared, reposted by fans, and live an evergreen life long after the show ends. Create opportunities for attendees to engage, curate, and even own content that you enable. Think of your booth as more than a destination; design it to be a launching pad for your best customers.

Technology used for designing and producing events is always changing. Be clear about your objectives, align your strategy with your objectives, and rely on expert professionals; if you do that, the technology will (almost) take care of itself.

ANTICIPATING WHAT'S NEXT: YOUR PRE-SHOW CHECKLIST

- Expand travel dates to include extra time around arrival and departure, allowing for exhibit setup and teardown schedules. These dates and times, as well as all related logistics, will most likely be dictated by the GSC responsible for getting exhibits in and out with minimal fuss.

- Prepare materials for shipment. Provide your carrier with pertinent show information such as the event and venue name, booth number, marshaling location, move-in times and dates, and move-out information. Make sure your shipment is properly packaged, labeled, and insured. Taking photos of freight before it ships is a good precaution and can help sort out any on-site issues.

- Using advance shipping ensures that packages arrive in time for move-in and eliminates needless worry when storms and other events delay transportation closer to the event date.

- Any shipments sent from the show back to your facility or on to the next show require a Material-Handling Agreement (MHA) with an outbound shipping provider experienced in load-out requirements. A bill of lading (BOL) is required to move the equipment off the show floor and transfer it to the outbound truck.

- Weigh your shipment prior to giving it to your carrier, and request that your carrier obtain a certified weight for your shipment to avoid delays and billing discrepancies.

- Ask your carrier about assessorial charges, waiting time fees, fuel surcharges, and other charges associated with trade show transportation. The original quote from a traditional carrier may exceed that of an official show carrier. Find out if your carrier will consolidate your shipment with other shipments, which can affect your target times, pickup times, and material-handling costs.

- Choose a carrier that will not split up your shipment in transit. Split shipments can lead to multiple material-handling charges rather than just one.

- Record all order confirmations and shipments with tracking numbers to reference on-site so that if a package is missing or mislaid, it can quickly be located.

- Schedule a pre-show meeting with your booth staff and any other company representatives attending the event so that you can go over show priorities, activations, contact information, and success goals and metrics.

- Before the event, create a post-show email that's ready to send once the show closes so that you can quickly respond to visitors and thank them for stopping by; use the opportunity to recap key messages and include a clear and enticing call to action.

PRO TIPS:

- The latest technology may be shiny and new, but it will add the most value if it actively supports the overall goals of your organization.

- Whether exhibitors hire professional presenters or deploy subject matter experts from their own company, it's important to train all booth personnel to perform as brand ambassadors. They are on the front line with the customers and their actions, demeanor, and appearance all reflect on the brand.

Note: Freight and material-handling considerations drive key budget and timeline decisions for every exhibitor. Refer to chapter 14, "Freight and Material-Handling Arrangements" on page 201 for more information about freight and material-handling arrangements and to chapter 15, "Exhibitors' On-Site Checklist" on page 212 for a complete exhibitor checklist.

BUILD THE PLAN

- Ask: How can we stay true to our mission, timeline, and budget?

- Clarify accountability. Hold a final team meeting prior to moving on-site to review the production schedule in detail with all teams, your last chance to address concerns and ensure safety and security contingencies are in place.

- Bring the approved event plan to life while working to reduce costs wherever possible and prevent errors.

- Know when to let these teams lead: operations, logistics, and production.

In this phase, everyone on the team shifts into high gear. The account lead for the agency should ask everyone on the team to document any time adjustments or build modifications that are required, in order to keep everything on time in budget, Documentation at this phase is essential to helping everyone learn from the process and informing your future plans.

CHAPTER 12

The Details of Producing the Show

TO-DO LIST:

- Review the event plan with the team members who will build and execute the event, focusing on the build timeline and its roles, responsibilities, task assignments, and due dates.

- Conduct a build phase kickoff meeting. Consider having the leads for the build phase, along with their project managers, deliver a presentation on how they will complete the build. Encourage helpful input from all parties to incorporate into the build plan.

- Double-check to ensure that safety, health, and security protocols are in place for load-in, the duration of the event, and load-out. Validate the crisis-management plan.

- Confirm all teams are on board with your ambient-wellness plan for each aspect of the event.

- Translate your event plan into spreadsheets, timelines, blueprints, schematics, renderings, CAD drawings, prototypes, production-ready graphics, permits, and specifications that spell out how each item must be designed, produced, equipped, transported, installed, deployed, and maintained.

- Conduct reviews with the whole team at key milestone dates, right through load-in.

Deliver with excellence. The fulfillment of your event plan depends on the successful management of the many details involved in the event build and show production efforts.

DETAILS, DETAILS, DETAILS

It cannot be overstated—be explicit in describing the details of each event component and leave nothing to interpretation. Case in point: Consider how many questions must be answered to produce a single banner. Assuming the basic artwork and approximate dimensions have already been presented and approved, those responsible for producing the banner still need to understand:

- Where will it be used (indoors/outdoors; does it need to be waterproof, heat sensitive)?

- How will it be suspended and from what (grommets, curtain rod, truss, Velcro)?

- What will it be made of (fabric, vinyl, a sustainable rigid substrate)?

- Should the graphic be designed for a full bleed, or should a margin accommodate hardware?

- What is the recommended resolution for the graphic?

- What kind of ink is most compatible for that material?

- Does it meet sustainability standards?

- Will the banner be repurposed?

- Will a single size and shape work everywhere, or should it have a modular design?

- What type of printing machine will best support all these prerequisites?

All of these questions and more must be answered for a single banner to go into production. Multiply that hundreds of times, and you'll begin to appreciate the scope of the build process for an entire event. Avoid costly do-overs and overtime fees by demanding explicit details.

Line up your A team. An event is only as good as the people making it happen. When the team pivots from planning the build to building the plan, conduct an official session with an agenda focused on making sure everyone's on the same page and has what they need to move forward. Whether you are the event manager running oversight on event progress or a member of the agency team working in the trenches, alignment of resources is a priority.

Event managers should be aware of the basic requirements, so they can hold their agency/GSC accountable for finding the right building materials, substrates, lumber, carpeting, furniture, and getting everything delivered to the venue as planned. This usually falls to the experts in logistics—the GSC—who may be part of the agency or a group contracted directly by the event creator. The logistics team will arrange for transportation and delivery of all the moving pieces, securing union contracts and special permits, plus arranging delivery of all exhibits and everything else required to stage the event.

For each of these major logistic concerns, someone needs to own responsibility for the budget, the timeline, and the expectations established in the creative proposal. This is generally owned by a lead person at the agency who is in daily contact with the event manager regarding status updates and any required change approvals.

Review the crisis management plan. This is the part of the event plan designed to address potential threats and hazards that could affect anyone working on show site. Even though this should have been distributed as part of the "Know Before You Go" communication, it's a best practice to review crisis concerns and mitigation plans in an onsite meeting with staff and crew as soon as possible. Each plan will be specific to the venue and the nature of the event.

Crisis management plans should include the following:

- Contact information—include name, title, email, and phone— for individuals representing the venue, show site leads, crisis team leads, AV team leads, agency team leads, and any corporate crisis team leads as appropriate. Be clear about who to call in each eventuality.

- List venue-specific crisis information:
    - Emergency numbers and phone lines
    - Evacuation emergency processes
    - Nonemergency numbers for reporting concerns
    - Where to find facility evacuation maps
    - Exits and routes needed for emergency evacuation
    - Safe refuge and/or evacuation reunification points in the event of an emergency—describe and indicate on a map
    - Communication plan to labor teams for exits, evacuation routes, and emergency plans
    - Attendee escalations should be handled with venue security/safety (e.g., trespassing, harassment, etc.)
    - Nearest hospital(s) and/or urgent care facility—name, address, hours, distance, and ER/ambulance services near the venue

- Emergency Mass Communications System—Identify what's in place with the event organizer or the lead service contractor.

- Emergency evacuation policy—Make it clear that all personnel/ staff will be guided by show management security, venue security, local enforcement and/or first responders.

- List potential threats and concerns—Identify any concerns specific to your location, timing, or event schedule. This could include precautions regarding hurricane season or how to keep people safe from heat stroke when working outdoors in direct sun. Be clear about the procedure to address or preempt each concern.

Identify any needed permits. Every event is unique and has different required permits depending on what's included and where the event is being held, which varies by city, county, and state. Some venues are already covered for local ordinances, but it's up to the event manager to double-check or rely on their agency or GSC to secure all permits. We've included a list of typical permits below for quick reference.

Commonly Required Permits

- **Alcoholic beverage consumption license**—This application process may require a long lead time depending on where and what you have planned. Find out if the venue where you are operating has a premises license, in which case you may be covered.

- **Building permits**—Any temporary outdoor structure, from bleachers and open pavilions or enclosed tents to huge staging areas, can require a building permit. (See temporary use and structure permit.) If you encroach on public space, you will need to secure additional permits, ranging from plaza/sidewalk permits, street activity (SAPO) permits, police permits, generator and electrical permits, red carpet permits, etc.

- **Business license**—Event management teams generally require proof of a business license in the contract agreement; it's a good practice, and suppliers should be prepared to provide licensing information.

- **Event permit**—Anyone organizing an event needs to check with the host city to secure permission. Note that the cost for the permit may be based on attendance.

- **Fire and pyrotechnics**—Given the potential for forest fires, outdoor fires and fireworks are often prohibited in the western states, and the fines are serious. Some venues make provisions for contained outdoor gas firepits that have already been approved. Indoor pyrotechnics are highly regulated; don't plan on making them part of your event before checking venue and fire marshal requirements and securing a permit.

- **Health permit**—If you plan to sell or serve food and/or beverages to the public at your event, a health permit will be required. Even providing free, prepackaged snacks at a networking area or passing out samples at an exhibit require a health permit. Food trucks also require special consideration for permitting.

- **Noise ordinances**—Outdoor events make noise. And even the loveliest concert must comply with the local ordinances, especially after dark. Plan to secure a noise permit and be prepared to go quiet—or switch to headphones—after 10 p.m.

- **Seller's permit**—If products are sold or leased at your event, the host state will want to collect sales tax. Make sure all suppliers and exhibitors engaged in actual sales have the required permits, which they may be required to display.

- **Temporary use and structure permit**—If you are staging some aspect of your event on vacant property, you'll need to secure the right permits, even if you're using it for staff parking, temporary structures (tents), loading areas, storage, or vendor equipment. Even if you have permission from the owner of private property, a permit is most likely required.

The event manager typically relies on the agency/GSC to produce the show, an effort led by an account lead or executive producer. They've already been overseeing weekly status meetings with the internal event team (to make sure everything is tracking on schedule and in budget) and status calls with the event manager's team. Communication between the event creator's personnel and its contracted partners and agencies is essential; the account lead for the agency or GSC usually acts as intermediary between the event manager and all contracted services.

Account leads will generally defer to the executive producer as planning shifts into building out the event. The executive producer then coordinates with the heads of the other teams in operations and logistics, exhibitor services, AV, graphic design, and any other groups involved. However, the roles of account lead and executive producer may be shared. Depending on the nature of the event plan, the account lead may oversee all the work that happens on the trade show floor or exhibition area, or they may share that with the executive producer. Generally, they work through the GSC's expo team, which is focused on logistics, including rigging, carpentry and exhibit installation, electrical connections, and even plumbing. A team dedicated to exhibitor services handles all the unique needs of those who have secured show floor booth space. Their designated lead most likely reports to the agency's account lead. The account lead then serves as the conduit between their team, the GSC, and the event manager.

Aspects of the event occurring outside the trade show floor (registration, the general session, breakouts, training sessions, immersion experiences, etc.) can be handled by a team reporting to the executive producer. Executive producers should know everything about the event and track it all in their playbook. Ask them any question (Who's going to inflate and position the faux palm trees for the Hawaiian picnic? Who will place the CEO's favorite brand of bottled water onstage? Who is pulling the required permits? How will the giant robot be loaded into position without anyone seeing?) and they'll have a plan for it in their playbook. No detail is too small to escape their notice. One of their key functions is mapping out assignments in an elaborate choreography so everything is covered, while remaining poised to swoop in whenever necessary to remove hurdles, offer coaching, and manage the unexpected things that event professionals learn to expect, helping the team stay focused on their assigned tasks by preempting disruptions.

Work the workflow. The agency or GSC manages a single workflow system that integrates all functions and enables everyone to track progress. One common workflow system allows everyone to see how things are progressing. The executive producer or account lead may assign a project manager to publish agendas and run weekly status meetings, keep the timeline up to date, and share relevant files securely in the team's preferred Cloud-based collaboration space.

Event creators may prefer a proprietary system behind the firewall of their organization, but typically the workflow is managed by the agency in a format that's secure while also being easy to share and accessible to all team members. The platform matters less than strict adherence to the process and protocols established by the team.

How the team approaches event production depends on the show itself. Each show's requirements are unique, but certain types of shows will feature similar workflows. For example, an annual trade show event will require a workflow that accommodates an exhibit hall or show floor set up for exhibitors, while a corporate event may be focused on products featured in gamification competitions with guest speakers, off-site networking, and other specialized experiences (and without a dedicated expo area).

Avoid the temptation to cut crew or take shortcuts to cut costs. Audiences (and stakeholders) remember the experience, not how much you saved. Savings won't cover the cost of an understaffed event. If attendees have to wait or failures occur, it sours the experience. Coverage of each moving part is essential.

Speech writers and coaches, choreographers, technical engineers, scenic designers, and all aspects of show production have roles that are dependent on others. Each aspect of the event will have a team lead, and that person needs to review all the deliverables and bring on any additional people required for their team's success on show day.

Clarify protocols. As the event draws near, make sure everyone is clear regarding any specific protocols, dress codes, or contingency plans. Review your established risk protocol—who to call in the event of an emergency, how to respond in a range of circumstances, how and when to isolate an incident and clear the area—with a complete contact sheet for all crew.

Plan for meals, breaks, snacks, water stations, coffee service, and any other foreseeable needs. The production schedule is designed around tightly scheduled food and meal breaks. For union crew members, the hours that can be worked are strictly regulated, and failure to meet them can bring steep penalties. But for any crew, union or otherwise, one of the ways you can show appreciation for their hard work and create a positive work environment is by taking care of their basic needs. The meals don't need to be fancy, but they should be filling, healthy, and accommodate food preferences (ex., vegetarian/vegan) and common allergies (ex., gluten/dairy). Making sure that there is a ready source of nourishment is a simple act of goodwill. Speaking pragmatically, if you have an electrical failure or the sound suddenly drops out, you don't want to rely on a hangry, disgruntled crew to find the problem and fix it.

A minimum of thirty minutes is expected for meal breaks that are served on-site. Although catering can seem costly, the advantage is that you don't lose anyone to traffic or other distractions, and the simple act of eating together is good for team building. If crew members are expected to go off-site and find their own meals, a minimum 45-minute break is required, and if there are no nearby eateries, you may need to extend this to an hour. Depending on the scope of the event and the build schedule, it may be advantageous to stagger the start time for breaks so that everyone on a large crew doesn't jump into the catering line (or local restaurant) all at once. Note that meal per diem rates are generally part of the contract with crew members. Be mindful of the budget impact of incurring meal penalties; if a client or presenter request puts the team in a meal penalty, they need to understand and authorize the budget impact.

AMBIENT WELLNESS

You have an obligation to implement basic health and wellness measures. Embrace KPIs that measure more than foot traffic and seek out other strategically relevant success metrics that support public health. Maintain the best practices most people are familiar with in the post-pandemic era: Antibacterial surface wipes at all counters, a robust cleaning schedule, and ubiquitous hand sanitizer stations will never go out of style. Control crowding and foot traffic pinch points. Take steps to improve air quality. No one wants to catch the flu and bring it home to their family. A little planning can go a long way toward prevention.

Healthier Registration

- Give attendees the option to register in advance via their tablet, computer, or smartphone.

- Germ-free, eco-friendly digital registration also supports data tracking and networking options and can also enable contactless pay.

- Badges can be digital, but if physical badges are preferred, offer to have them mailed out in advance and/or create print-from-home options.

- Provide staggered check-in times.

- Create satellite check-in stations at convenient places (such as the airport or host hotels) to give attendees a crowd-free experience while better serving their needs.

Logistics on the Floor

- Stay mindful of how you can use your event design to allow for casual social distancing.

- Think about how to keep surface germs from spreading. Enable touch-free doors and entryways.

- Walk around the event venue and look for potential pinch points. Get creative in imagining other ways to prevent attendees from creating human logjams.

- Promoting remote viewing rooms around the perimeter of your general session theater can help guests avoid uncomfortable crowding.

- Offer satellite versions of high-traffic attractions (morning coffee stations, charging stations, wellness experiences) to help disperse traffic and avoid crowd formation.

Exhibitor Services Center

Consider how your exhibitor services center works. If the first touch point takes the form of a live virtual consultant, many problems can be solved remotely. If necessary, the service person can make an appointment to provide further assistance, preventing unnecessary bunching up at the service desk. Chatbot and AI-driven service is a good option for supporting exhibitors and attendees alike. Voice-based interactive systems provide a quick and cost-effective way to answer questions and request services. Everyone benefits from the improved efficiency and reduced person-to-person interaction that minimizes the spread of germs.

Signage

Many events now feature wellness information on signage maps, indicating the location of hand-sanitation stations and medical check-in rooms.

Everyone appreciates wellness stations that offer temperature detection and N95 masks to those who develop a cough or sneeze during the event; ensure signage points to these locations.

On the Show Floor

Think about how your layout supports or detracts from traffic flow and healthy interaction. Consider some of these tactics to help ensure a healthier show floor experience.

- You're probably already creating wider aisles and spacing between booths. Once the show is up and running, the use of heat maps to determine crowd density, NFC data, or beacons that show foot traffic can promote ambient wellness by mitigating overcrowding.

- For each of your attendee personas, curate recommended pathways that take them where they want to go without clogging up main throughfares.

- Consider indicating one-way aisle traffic with signage or staff members on hand to help control crowd density.

- Make sure that large touch screens and wearable tech like VR headsets follow sanitation protocols.

- Set up roving robots or staff on scooters carrying live-feed video cameras offering a real-time look at floor activity. This video can be shared and used to immerse virtual audiences in the event while providing in-person attendees with a preview of action on the floor, so they can prioritize their choices based on personal interest and traffic flow.

- Schedule docent-led tours of the show floor during which aisles are cleared of casual traffic. Complement these tour times with windows during which exhibitors schedule visits by appointment only. Among other benefits, this practice enables immuno-compromised attendees to conduct business without undo fear of contagion.

Promote the use of virtual application-based systems that allow attendees to identify points of interest on their smartphones and be more efficient with their time moving from place to place. Encourage practices that rely on attendees using their own devices to experience digital connections and receive notifications and other event information.

PRO TIPS:

- Conduct a final walk-through of the venue to confirm that all setups, decorations, and technical equipment are in place and functioning correctly.

- Maintain open communication with vendors and staff through-out the event to swiftly address any last-minute changes or concerns.

- Establish a designated relaxation area for staff to recharge and stay hydrated during breaks to prevent burnout.

- Display clear signage indicating designated smoking areas, and remind attendees to respect local ordinances regarding smoking.

- Familiarize yourself with the venue's evacuation procedures, and communicate them to staff and attendees in case of emergency.

- Schedule regular breaks and encourage attendees to participate in physical activities or mindfulness exercises to promote mental and physical wellness.

- Arrange transportation options for attendees, such as shuttle services or rideshare partnerships, to promote responsible drinking and ensure safe travel home.

- Designate a quiet space for attendees who may need a break from the noise and stimulation of the event.

- Ensure that all performers and presenters have the necessary permits and licenses to avoid legal complications during the event. (For example, a video soundtrack that has been licensed for use in internal meetings may not meet ASCAP licensing requirements if you plan to livestream the event.)

- Coordinate with local medical services to have medical professionals on standby in case of medical emergencies.

- Establish a clear communication plan with staff and volunteers, including designated channels for reporting emergencies and incidents.

- Implement a comprehensive security plan, including bag checks and crowd control measures, to ensure the safety of attendees and staff.

- Provide clear instructions for attendees on what to do in case of emergency, including evacuation routes and emergency contact information.

- Be planning for and thinking about the debriefing session you've scheduled after the event to discuss what went well and areas for improvement, allowing for continuous learning and refinement of future events.

CHAPTER 13

Making Presentations More Meaningful

> ## TO-DO LIST:
>
> - Conduct regularly scheduled status update meetings and get input on progress.
>
> - Rehearse all presentations to ensure that the people onstage, as well as show crew and tech operators, are prepared.
>
> - Confirm any necessary revisions or deviation requests that arise with the team and decision-makers; note impacts to budget and timeline.
>
> - Test or rehearse any new processes, key elements, or techniques as well as those that are unusual for the presenters or crew.

Plan ahead for successful presentations. Start out by considering the needs of those who'll be presenting on your stage. Every event has unique needs for its general session or "main stage" headliners. Whether the onstage presenters are executives from the event manager's own company, guests scheduled through a speaker's bureau, or professionals responding to a call for papers, treat them with respect by making sure they are prepared and properly supported. Early and consistent communication is key.

Check to see if they have any dietary, health, or security requirements. If you'll have walk-on music (bursts of song that play while a presenter walks onstage), find out if they have a favorite or signature song. If you're working with a professional talent coordinator who contracts paid performers, they will scrutinize the rider (special requirements) and make sure everything is in place.

Presenters and performers need to know the time and place to show up for rehearsals and sound checks. On show day, they need to know the plan for fitting them with a microphone. You need to know if they require a lectern or if they prefer an open stage. Are they bringing their own speaker-support visuals, or are you providing them? Do they need to use your slide template? Have you communicated screen formats, resolution issues, etc.?

Designate a green room, the place where presenters relax prior to appearing onstage. If your presenters are entering from the front of house, be sure the production team knows to reserve front row seats nearest the stage steps. Always arrange to have a small high-top table onstage preset with enough water bottles for each presenter; identify a stagehand who will reset these at each break.

You can offer to have the production team advance their visuals, but many professional speakers prefer to advance the slides themselves with a pickle switch while watching a confidence monitor (showing what's on the screen and, sometimes, the next visual). Double-check to ensure their visual format is compatible with yours; offer to manage any required conversion. Prior to rehearsal, do a test run to make sure all content is show ready.

Working with a teleprompter. Professional teleprompter equipment and operators should be provided for all staged presentations. This is especially important for executive presenters who, unlike professional speakers, won't have a lot of time to become familiar with their scripts. It can be challenging to get time with a busy executive, but if they frequently stumble during an important presentation, it can inadvertently erode trust; audiences like to see a confident, relaxed presenter. That ability comes from experience but also from familiarity with the material and practice working with the script.

Originally, teleprompter setups relied on "presidential monitors," small glass panels on either side of a lectern that the presenter could use to follow the script while looking through the glass to the audience. This works but also locks the presenter to the lectern. LED monitors or, for video broadcasts, TV-style monitors mounted to the primary camera are more commonly used now. Teleprompter packages vary, but the package to cover all contingencies is one that includes floor confidence monitors near the front of the stage and large monitors in the back of the room. These back-of-house monitors can be raised on platform stands or hung from the ceiling. This allows the presenter to maintain eye contact with the audience, which is especially critical if the presentation is being recorded or livestreamed; without them, your presenter will be forced to look down, and your video will feature the top of a talking head.

If live presentations will also be broadcast, priority must be given to the speakers' on-screen appearance. Placing teleprompter monitors in the back of the room helps ensure presenters make eye contact with the camera's audience. Use lavalier microphones or position stand mics so they don't interfere visually. Position the presenter so that the set or background visuals don't result in an unfortunate appearance or distract from their message.

The professional teleprompter operator usually sits backstage in the production area near the team punching the slides and running video playback. The operator will follow the presenter's lead, which is why it is important for them to rehearse together. Many executive presenters tend to race when they speak, so it helps to adjust how the script appears on the monitor—by spacing out sentences, adding ellipses between words, or bumping up the font size—to help presenters find a better rhythm. As they rehearse, they may find that it helps to replace awkward words or simplify messaging. Make sure your production schedule includes time for every presenter to rehearse with the teleprompter operator who will be running the equipment on show day.

When changes are made during rehearsal or on-site, have the writer or script supervisor keep track of what's changed and then incorporate those edits into the prompter. The script coordinator must also make sure the show caller and graphics crew are aware of any changes.

Consider using off-site rehearsals. Depending on the activities that will happen at the event, it often makes sense to hold your initial rehearsals at an off-site location. This gives everyone time and a stress-free environment in which to work out any presentation bugs before the team moves into the venue and onto the stage.

For example, if there will be press events, elaborate demonstrations, choreographed movement, product reveals, or entertainment extravaganzas taking place on the show floor, it's good to let presenters practice the speech elsewhere first, possibly at the vendor's facility. That way, any coaching for executive presenters, changes to scripts, teleprompter layout, and AV support can be worked out before more costly on-site rehearsal time, where your crew/labor rates will quickly add up.

Busy executives are hard-pressed for time and often delegate the content of their presentation to someone else; that's fine until they find themselves onstage in a dress rehearsal, delivering their presentation for the first time. By scheduling an off-site dress rehearsal a week before the show, you're opening space in the executive's calendar to focus on the presentation. As necessary, you can capture changes at that time and still have time to adjust and polish visuals.

Make sure rehearsal isn't cannibalizing the limited time your production team has to do their work. Considering the need to manage labor hour costs and respect other production schedule mandates, it makes sense to plan ahead and offline any rehearsals that don't absolutely need to happen on-site. Try to preempt any timing conflicts by letting presenters know the rehearsal schedule early, for both off-site and onstage rehearsals. Off-site rehearsals need to be included in the budget. In addition to the teleprompter operator, writers and/or script managers, you may want to include a speaker coach, off-site room producer, A/V support, equipment rental, room rental, refreshments, and hair and makeup.

TRAINING AND CERTIFICATION

Training and certification sessions are prime attractions for association events that cater to those required to update their professional development requirements. Many associations have personnel in charge of training, and they work with instructional designers to develop the actual curriculum.

For your organization or client, if certification means reviewing material on a computer and then being tested, research suggests that it's best to offer examinations virtually, before or after your live show. Why make people travel to do something they can more easily and inexpensively do from home?

For live-and-in-person events, design your training session with the same care you'd give any other mainstage event or breakout session. Make it interactive. Support the presenters with the tools and technology they need. Feature hands-on practice, veteran-to-newbie mentoring, physical demonstrations, and testimonials from experts. Design for immersion, interaction, and audience participation, especially if your audience consists of professionals who may be able to share insights that could benefit the rest of the group.

PRO TIPS:

- Triple-check all presentation materials to ensure they're in the correct order and formatted correctly for smooth transitions.

- Familiarize speakers with the teleprompter well in advance to ensure they're comfortable and confident during their presentations.

- Conduct off-site rehearsals to simulate the actual event environment, and iron out any logistic or technical issues beforehand.

- Use off-site rehearsals to fine-tune stage layouts and lighting for optimal visibility and ambiance, and to coordinate speaker cues, timing, and stage movements for a seamless flow during the live event.

- Provide thorough training on using teleprompters, including troubleshooting common issues that may arise during live presentations. Optimize teleprompter speed to match the presenter's speaking pace for a natural and polished delivery.

- Develop comprehensive scripts for teleprompter use, including cues for pauses, emphasis, and transitions, to maintain a natural speaking rhythm.

- Incorporate interactive elements into presentations to engage attendees and keep their attention throughout the event.

- Implement feedback mechanisms during off-site rehearsals to gather input from presenters and make necessary adjustments before the event.

- Collaborate closely with translators to ensure accurate and timely interpretation services for multilingual presentations at association events.

- Use off-site rehearsals to troubleshoot potential language barriers and ensure seamless integration of translation services into the event program.

- Create visually appealing graphics and scenic properties that align with the event's theme and messaging to enhance the presentations and ambient room design.

- Incorporate off-site rehearsals into the design process to test the visibility and impact of graphics and 3D properties in different lighting and viewing conditions.

CHAPTER 14

Think Big, Act Small

TO-DO LIST:

- Anticipate the fire marshal's expectations and proactively deliver what's needed.

- Ensure that fabrication and logistics teams are in lockstep.

- Coordinate freight and material-handling arrangements in advance to ensure timely delivery and efficient distribution of supplies and equipment.

- Work closely with vendors and suppliers to coordinate delivery schedules and ensure that materials and equipment arrive on time and in good condition.

- Scrutinize production and installation plans for all graphics—signs, banners, LED displays, floor decals, etc.—to ensure everything is on track.

- Ensure that exhibitor services personnel are aware of and managing any exhibitor concerns, prioritizing those that impact the larger load-in plan.

Building out an event happens on multiple levels. The team managing logistics, usually a GSC, will create a package of documents that update the finished event plan, literally detailing how all the moving pieces will get to the venue and be loaded in and installed, and then all the same detail in reverse for load-out. This master build plan must contain all the tiny pieces that have been detailed in graphic layouts, blueprints, rental agreements—anywhere. As the build progresses, the master plan must be updated, with confirmation that all the components of the plan still work together. The process starts big but becomes increasingly granular as work begins and all aspects are defined, down to the tiniest details. Responsibility for execution and delivery then shifts to an array of people who build, rent, and purchase whatever it takes to make the build plan "real."

FILE PLANS WITH THE FIRE MARSHAL

Safety is a priority; compliance with safety regulations must be reflected in all plans. Final CAD plans must be submitted to the local fire marshal (the person assigned to your venue who has authority to approve your event plans—or not). They will expect your CAD plans to show the placement of all equipment and furniture, the width of aisles, how many doors per expected attendee, visible exit signs, ingress and egress routes from the building, and more. An experienced GSC will file plans at least three weeks ahead of the show's opening date and would never plan to use pyrotechnics without thoroughly understanding the restrictions in place at the event venue. Schedule a live walk-through of the event with the fire marshal on the day before the show opens and be prepared for feedback; it's not unusual for them to demand certain modifications, which will not be optional. Fire marshals are authorized to shut down any event for any reason, so working to ensure early compliance is better for everyone.

The rules vary depending on each city and venue, but here are some things to plan for:

- Obtain certification that your design relies on furniture and decorative materials that are certified as fireproof or treated with flame retardant. The fire marshal may ask to see these certificates, which the GSC should be prepared to show.

- Don't block or obscure doors, exit signs, fire hoses, or emergency strobe lights. In the event of a fire or loss of power, the emergency exit signs will be the only way people have of finding their way out.

    - Many producers include extra battery-powered exit signs as part of their production equipment, just to play it safe.

    - It is sometimes possible to receive advance permission from the fire marshal to cover an exit door. If this is part of your plan, make sure that the emergency exit sign for the door is also covered so that if there is an emergency, no one runs toward a blocked exit.

    - Show that there is no cabling going across the egress doors and that, in the event of a fire, there is nothing that will interfere with fire hoses or ceiling sprinklers.

- Observe specific safety requirements relating to covered and closed rooms in an exhibit space, subject to fire marshal approval. Fire extinguishers and smoke detectors are required. Large rooms may require a sprinkler system.

- Make sure that all vehicles associated with your event are parked in designated areas that do not block fire hydrants or the routes that would be used by fire, police, and EMS trucks. There are specific rules that need to be followed if a vehicle is to be displayed on the show floor or stage.

Learn as much as you can about local regulations, work with the venue to discover any specific things that have been issues in the past, and engage with the fire marshal as a willing partner. Double-check that you have all the required permits. Some demands may seem trivial, painful, or costly, but the fire marshal will be holding you accountable for preventing the loss of life. There's no argument—only compliance.

FABRICATION

Whether an event is hosted by a large corporate entity putting together their own show, by a for-profit show organizer hoping to attract trade professionals, or an association selling exhibit space to businesses that cater to their members, the physical focal point is generally a branded display structure of some sort—an exhibit, booth, theatrical staging area, or permanent installation. Someone needs to build it all, and that's where fabrication comes into play.

A custom experience can be created by renting modular pieces and fitting them with graphics, a great option for many business models. But a bespoke, custom-built exhibit requires a skilled, experienced fabrication team. These carpenters, machinists, finishers, painters, and packaging experts know the ins and outs of building materials for events, expos, market activations, theater-quality props and scenic components, and permanent installations.

Most operations also have the ability to create custom containers for shipping exhibit pieces and have maintenance and storage capabilities. This team should also understand how to create competitive estimates for all its custom work by collaborating with pipeline experts to secure the best materials and pricing possible, sourcing the most advantageous locations (depending on the final destination).

Fabrication shops are also skilled in properly labeling each skid so that, upon arrival, the team assembling the exhibit knows which to open first and can ensure that all items have been accounted for. Packaging and labeling are critical; there's nothing worse for an exhibitor than learning that something's missing.

Project management is essential, especially as fabrication shops tend to work on multiple projects at any given time. The build plan for every exhibit works backward from the precise time a delivery truck must pull into a specific dock in the required venue, where it will be loaded in and installed. The project manager keeps the build on track and acts as liaison with the rest of the event team. A fabrication team that is part of the agency's or GSC's operation facilitates efficient planning, tracking, management, and execution of the work.

LARGE-FORMAT GRAPHICS AND PRINT CONSIDERATIONS

Giant floor decals, hanging ceiling-to-floor banners, and simple seat-assignment cards are all printed using different equipment. The designer responsible for preparing the files will understand how each piece is being printed and will prepare the files accordingly. Get your graphics orders in early! Give your team plenty of time to make sure everything is ready to go. Double-check your order inventory and ensure the indicated on-site placement for each item is correct.

Once these files are turned over for printing, a staff expert will add some machine-specific technical data and prepare the substrate material being printed to optimize its appearance and durability. They will consider whether the item will be repurposed or recycled. The image could be printed on plastic, glass, paper, vinyl, canvas, or other materials; the printer is the ultimate expert on how each material accepts the ink and how long it takes to cure.

Printing can be a labor-intensive process that requires sewing, fitting grommets, and preparing fabrics to be mounted to special framing hardware on-site. Sustainability goals are a factor here, as some materials and inks are more environmentally friendly than others. The quality of sustainable materials and processes is always improving, and your printer may have some recommendations that can be effectively implemented if you ask early enough in the process.

When the printer prepares the finished materials to be shipped to the show site, make sure they include photos with unpacking and mounting instructions. Large agencies/GSCs may have their own in-house printing; that gives event managers an added level of confidence, knowing the people responsible for preparing the graphic files, print-ing, shipping, and installing the materials all work together using a common process and shared timeline.

LED SIGNAGE

Relying on LED signage for everything, from major displays to directional signage, simplifies the production process while bringing considerable benefits in terms of sustainability. If a venue offers fixed LED monitors for wayfinding and agenda boards outside of each room, you can cus-tomize your event in an environmentally responsible way. The content on LED signs can usually be programmed to change on-site as your agenda unfolds or to highlight special events or support contingency announcements, such as room changes.

Each set of LED images must be created by a graphic designer who can ensure the files have the correct resolution, brightness, and aspect ratio. The designer will also try to match colors between print and digital media. While the RGB (red-green-blue) color mode is used for digital images displayed on a screen (from smartphones to jumbotrons), the CMYK (cyan-magenta-yellow-black) color mode is used for designs that are printed. Because of the differences in how our eyes see projected or digital color and how we see reflective, printed color, work with graphic designers who understand how to optimize both.

A WORD TO EXHIBITORS: FINALIZING YOUR PLAN

If you're an exhibitor at a trade show, your exhibit or booth is the hub from which you'll be packaging an experience that captures the attention of your target audience. Success at a single show can pay huge dividends for the entire fiscal year. The show organizer retains an exhibitor services group to wrangle everything related to the exhibition floor; they can help you design an exhibit from scratch or simply work with you to arrange load-in and load-out details. Fabrication shops may also have the ability to transport, store, and maintain your exhibit, if desired. Coordinate with exhibitor services to make sure all your materials, including the exhibit, are shipped on schedule and delivered on time to your designated exhibit space within the venue.

Freight and Material-Handling Arrangements

New exhibitors may be surprised to learn about distinct fees for shipping the materials to the venue and for loading them from the dock to the exhibit space. These costs are driven by weight and require certified weight tickets (another form you'll find in the exhibitor kit). Because hundreds of exhibitors will be sending myriad containers, the process for maintaining order is pretty rigorous. It all needs to be coordinated with the assigned exhibitor services team, who have support staff trained to help guide exhibitors through the requirements, often dictated by strict union regulations.

Inbound shipping refers to the transport of exhibit materials to the venue's warehouse or dock; *outbound shipping* refers to sending the exhibit to its next destination (another event or a storage facility). Watch out for special handling fees that can be incurred for freight that's not properly packaged. Make sure your exhibit house understands the requirements and alerts you if, in fact, your materials will require special handling.

Ship materials to a storage warehouse near the final destination well in advance of the actual date for loading into the venue. With limited time to get everyone onto the show floor, it's wise to organize your materials off-site to expedite the actual load-in time at the venue.

Material handling includes a list of services: unloading exhibit materials, storing them for up to thirty days in advance of the show in a warehouse, delivering them to the booth, storing empty containers during the event, returning the containers for repacking, and reloading the freight onto outbound carriers when the event closes. Material handling should not be confused with shipping exhibit materials to and from the event, as both services typically have separate charges.

Your exhibitor kit should provide target freight information requirements, which are especially important for large events with multiple venues. Selecting a carrier familiar with trade show protocols can save you time and money; consider using the official show carrier to eliminate extra fees and surcharges.

Exhibitors who want to carry their own materials into the venue will quickly learn that at many large conference centers it's not allowed; the union will handle it. Likewise, even seemingly simple equipment setups may require, by contract, a union electrician. While this may seem like an imposition at the time, it protects all exhibitors from someone going rogue, blowing fuses, creating a traffic hazard, or, worse, starting an electrical fire that puts everyone at risk. Exhibitors should also expect to pay for electricity used; utility costs and even internet connections may or may not be baked into your fee.

Work with the exhibitor services staff to make sure materials are delivered without a hitch, union protocols are respected, and exhibitors have budgeted for surprise costs. Keep a detailed inventory of what's being shipped and what skid/pallet number each item is on. Photos can help the team on the ground locate shipments that might go missing. Understanding safe and efficient transport is critical to your success. Planning ahead will help you better prepare for your show while giving you the peace of mind that comes with knowing where your exhibit is at all times. Familiarity with the following terms can help exhibitors navigate the process and achieve superior results.

SHIPPING AND HANDLING GLOSSARY

- **Advance warehouse**—Location to receive freight before start of show. Freight is stored at this location and then moved to the event at the designated time.

- **Bill of lading (BOL)**—A legal document issued by a carrier (transportation company) to a shipper that details the type, quantity, and destination of the goods being carried; required for all shipments that need to arrive and depart the exhibit hall.

- **Cart service**—A flat rate material-handling service that assigns laborers to exhibitors to unload or load their personal vehicles. The service is meant to support smaller exhibitors and typically has a weight or time limit outlined in the event information.

- **Crated or uncrated shipments**—Crated shipments include material packed in any type of shipping container that can be unloaded at the dock with no additional handling required. This includes crates, fiber cases, cartons, and properly packed skids. Uncrated materials refer to those shipped loose or pad-wrapped, and/or moved using unskidded machinery (without the proper lifting bars or hooks typically required by a forklift).

- **Dark day**—Any day during move-in or move-out of the facility when event services are shut down, such as on a holiday.

- **Double time labor**—The pay rate for work performed that's double the normal hourly rate, generally because the demand for work extends beyond agreed-upon workday hours, or possibly on weekends or holidays (see overtime labor).

continued

- **Exhibitor services center**—A centralized area where representatives of various event services can be contacted or located on-site at an event (also referred to as the *service desk*).

- **Material-Handling Agreement (MHA)**—An official outbound shipping authorization form that allows freight to be released to a chosen carrier after the event concludes.

- **Material handling**—The service and cost of transporting exhibit materials and related items from the truck at the loading dock to their designated location on the show floor, then removing and storing crates until they are returned for load-out.

- **Overtime labor**—Typically, work performed before 8:00 a.m. and after 4:30 p.m., Monday through Friday, and all hours on Saturdays, Sundays, and holidays (varies by city).

- **Privately owned vehicle**—A car, van, or other passenger vehicle primarily designed to move people, referred to as *POVs*. The term is used to distinguish personal vehicles from box trucks, tractor trailers, and other vehicles whose purpose is to move freight.

- **Special handling**—Materials delivered in such a manner that requires additional handling, such as ground unloading, stacked and constricted space unloading, designated piece unloading, loads mixed with pad-wrapped material, loads failing to maintain shipping integrity, carpet and/or pad-only shipments, and shipments that require additional time, equipment, or labor to unload. Typically, FedEx and UPS handling are included in this category due to their delivery procedures.

- **Straight time labor**—The hours considered normal business hours (see overtime labor).

- **Target date**—The specified date and time to move into and/ or out of an exhibit hall or venue.

Successful event planning and execution require meticulous attention to detail across multiple levels, from the initial design and fabrication considerations to the practicalities of print, LED signage strategies, and exhibitor services. Coordinating with authorities like the fire marshal and ensuring smooth freight and material handling arrangements are vital components of ensuring a seamless, successful event day.

Before we get deeper into the build, try incorporating these pro tips into your planning process to optimize the attendee experience and maximize the impact of your event.

PRO TIPS:

- Prioritize filing your plans with the fire marshal early in the process to avoid last-minute complications or delays on the day of the event.

- Never assume that an exhibit that works in one venue will work in another; double-check schematics and diagrams and be aware of local fire marshal requirements and prepared for inspection day.

- Pay attention to fabrication considerations such as material durability and ease of assembly to streamline setup and minimize potential issues during the event.

- Utilize LED signage to display real-time updates, schedules, and announcements; leverage design cues to keep attendees informed and engaged throughout the event.

- Leverage LED signage to showcase sponsors, partners, and advertisers, providing them with valuable exposure and recognition.

- Implement a streamlined process for exhibitors to request and access additional services or support during the event, ensuring their needs are met promptly and efficiently.

CHAPTER 15

Aspects of the Build

TO-DO LIST:

- Coordinate with venue staff ahead of time to streamline the load-in process and avoid any logistical hiccups on opening day.

- Create a detailed timeline for load-in, ensuring each team member knows their responsibilities and deadlines to maintain efficiency.

- Conduct a pre-conference meeting to check show-ready status with all team leaders.

- Troubleshoot registration software and equipment.

- Implement a contingency plan for unexpected challenges during load-in, such as inclement weather or traffic delays.

- Train registration staff to efficiently handle last-minute, on-site registrations and address any attendee inquiries with professionalism and courtesy.

- Implement mobile check-in options to reduce wait times and accommodate attendees who prefer digital registration methods.

- Offer personalized assistance at the registration desk to cater to the unique needs of each attendee and exceed their expectations.

The agency or GSC acts as the show management's right-hand partner in making sure everything is prepared for a smooth load-in and successful opening day of the planned event. As the exclusive provider of rigging, furniture rental, signage, labor, carpet, displays, transportation, and material handling, the agency or GSC is responsible for making sure things run like clockwork. In some cases, other contractors may provide AV, electrical, and utilities services, which will have been decided earlier. The agency will be familiar with any specific venue requirements and vendor contracts. Everyone involved in the event should be in daily contact.

A detailed build schedule will account for only so many trucks showing up in a given time span (determined by the number of loading docks), essentially building from the ground up and the ceiling down. The team will map out each booth or exhibit area on the show floor, run electrical wires and basic rigging, install carpeting, and do everything that must happen before the exhibits are rolled in. Regarding collective bargaining agreements, any number of unions may be represented at a given event, and their contracts must all be honored. Make sure everyone on the event team understands the parameters of the union agreements so that no one inadvertently causes a hiccup.

THE PRE-CON MEETING

As the event date moves closer, activity associated with the event build becomes more intense. The production schedule should work like a playbook to spell out in minute detail everything that needs to happen in the five to seven days prior to the official load-in day. Typically, the frequency of production team meetings has tightened, now happening on a daily basis. Approximately one week prior to load-in, hold a final official meeting between all meeting planners, all agency team leads, and representatives of the host facility.

Each event will drive its own pre-con meeting agenda, but here are some things typically considered:

- An overview of the event, including confirmation of responsibilities for all vendors and the interface between the agency, other contractors, and venue-exclusive services

- The floor plan and carpet plans, noting any changes

- Any factors relating to the exhibitors' experience, from freight issues, service desk hours, electrical and internet needs to cleaning times

- Any special needs related to decorating or off-property deliveries

- A production update on any special structural systems— from the registration desk to unique experiential setups

- Exhibit status, how many work tickets and custom booths are expected, and whether there are any issues or additional orders that must be accounted for

- Fabrication status, including the date drivers hit the road and are expected to make their deliveries

- Graphics and deployment/installation with a review of who is printing, when things can be expected on-site, the process for flagging damaged goods, and any outstanding issues

- Freight updates in terms of delivery times, labor factors, warehouse timeliness, marshaling yard hours, and other potential issues

- Transportation specific to the management and delivery of exhibit materials

- Rigging issues, ranging from height limitations on the show floor to equipment needs to priorities of the show management team

continued

- Electrical issues, from any special requirements for the AV team managing the general session to individual exhibitor concerns

- Internet requirements, including everything needed for dedicated product demos, unique passwords for the event teams and attendees, and confirmed date of installation

- GSC management issues relating to the facility, labor, fire marshal inspections, problematic road construction or closures, and measures taken to ensure security and safety

- Protocols for team communication and feedback capture

- A rigorous review of the production schedule

THE LOWDOWN ON LOAD-IN

Loading an event into a convention center requires a variety of logistic tools and processes to make sure things stay on track. Online systems allow everyone to access the plan, track progress, and coordinate activity from their phone. This saves valuable time on-site, when a round-trip walk from the loading dock to the registration area adds up to half a mile.

Logistics is everything. Each discrete task has been assigned a job ticket and moves forward in a logical order. For example, logistics experts may decide to set up the back walls of the registration area but wait to set up the desks and counters, based on other demands for equipment and crews in that space. If loading docks are limited, the requirements of one crew may need to be balanced with those building the general session experience. All activity is choreographed for optimum efficiency, protecting the fit and finish of exhibit materials, preventing do-overs, and avoiding wasted motion.

The GSC account lead, often working with the agency's executive producer or other core team members, will walk through the venue with the organizer's meeting planners to assess how things are progressing every day before the show officially opens. The team will go through the production schedule and conduct a level-set, compare notes, and see if everything is progressing on schedule or if adjustments need to be made. At this point, problems with graphic production or pipeline delays can get expensive, so the team may create work-around plans to keep labor engaged and avoid falling behind. The event manager often attends these meetings and may be asked to approve overtime or the realignment of resources to keep things on track.

THE REGISTRATION DESK

Functioning more as a concierge service, the registration desk may still be the place to hand out name badges and handle last-minute on-site registrations. Your staff should think like attendees and prepare to anticipate attendee needs, questions, and expectations.

Before your guests arrive, double-check that your registration software is working, all your staff know how to use it, and they know who to call if anything goes amiss. Make sure you have reliable Wi-Fi and a backup plan, so all required files can be accessed offline. If you're printing badges or anything else on-site, don't rely on Wi-Fi; rather, connect directly to a dedicated printer. If there is anything you can do the day before the show opens, do it. Prepare your team with useful answers to FAQs. Have backup plans for anything that could go wrong. Do whatever you can to make the experience more pleasant for attendees.

The registration desk is usually located front and center at an event—prime real estate—but once an event is underway, this area can look like a ghost town. Think about how to repurpose this area after the registration rush while still providing basic coverage. Perhaps the desk can be reduced to a simple kiosk or small concierge-type stand, and the rest of the space can be used to stage a sponsored reception or special exhibit. The ability to keep changing the face of your event pays dividends. You may find that repurposing this area leads to a new revenue stream.

PRO TIPS:

- Utilize technology such as RFID badges or QR code scanners to streamline the registration process and minimize manual data entry errors.

- Provide VIP attendees with expedited registration services to enhance their experience and demonstrate white-glove service.

- Train registration staff to upsell additional event features or merchandise to maximize revenue opportunities and enhance attendee engagement.

- Provide complimentary amenities at the registration desk, such as water bottles or branded merchandise, to enhance the attendee experience and leave a lasting impression.

- Anticipate and address common attendee concerns or questions proactively to minimize wait times and ensure a smooth registration process.

- Implement a queuing system at the registration desk to manage crowds effectively and prevent bottlenecks during peak registration periods.

EXHIBITORS' ON-SITE CHECKLIST

- Before the show opens, check your space to ensure all shipments have arrived, and confirm all orders have been completed or are in process.

- If you hired labor (for setup, installations, power, etc.), check in at the service desk to ensure your work order is in process. While you're there, confirm teardown labor, too.

- Locate your booth on the exhibit floor. Confirm the orientation of the booth is correct, and have the booth chalked for installation.

- Electrical wiring is the first item for placement, so confirm it is run to the correct location prior to any carpet or floor installation. Once the floor is installed, the exhibit build will proceed.

- When your booth is up and you've placed all your materials, demo equipment, props, etc., walk down the aisle. Step away from your booth and look around to make sure nothing is blocking your booth signage from any angle.

- Check the traffic: Think about how people will walk through your booth—keep comfortable social distancing in mind—and position your key messages in areas where most visitors will linger.

- Test, test, test! Make sure all equipment and any digital activations (such as your lead capture, appointment scheduling, and CRM tools) are working properly before show opening. Likewise, familiarize yourself with all available event technologies. You may have chat bots, event platforms, exhibitor-support apps, and other event management software to feed into your CRM platform and help you get more value out of your trade show investment.

- Empty boxes and containers should all be labeled right away—before teardown—so that they can be easily retrieved. Just as important, make sure you've removed everything you might need for the show, because once boxes are moved to storage, you won't have access to them until after the event, for load-out.

- Make sure you have an item count and identify which pallets you need returned first. (Each show has different guidelines, but you can usually have a certain number of prioritized "first back" pallets to expedite load-out.) After the show, collect all final leads, business cards, and notes gathered from staff during the show.

- Depending on booth size and complexity, you may designate a point person or vendor to oversee teardown, material packing, and shipping.

continued

- Complete a Material-Handling Agreement for all outbound shipments (each destination requires its own MHA), and return it to the exhibitor service center when you have all pallets ready for pickup. The people at the service desk will summon the truck so teamsters can load your shipment, but everything must be ready at that time.

- Apply labels to every container and/or box you plan to ship. Help the teamsters by labeling each to include both the individual item number and the total number (i.e., 1 of 15, 2 of 15, etc.).

- Ask the service desk and hired vendors for all final invoices.

- Evaluate your success at the show according to the goals you set for this event and your planned ROI metrics. Conduct an on-site or post-show survey to gauge the effectiveness of the marketing campaign and in-booth activations. Survey your team and customers to improve your next show.

- Follow up with leads and contacts to keep the conversation going. Make sure the correspondence happens no later than a week following the event.

UNDERSTANDING CORPORATE EXHIBITORS

Corporations sending massive displays to select events will have different expectations from the typical trade show exhibitor. While the overall design, build, and shipping process is the same, corporations have strict brand guidelines that must be followed. The event properties must dovetail with a brand's larger marketing plan, deliver on highly defined metrics, and meet a higher set of standards. Corporate clients expect full-service custom solutions to fully engage their audiences and drive them to action, requiring personalized service, with a dedicated account lead, project manager, and design/creative team.

Corporate event managers invest heavily in the event and expect white-glove service. They don't typically work on an annual planning cycle, because they have a portfolio of events and go-to-market activations to manage. Market-driven corporate events often work on shorter lead times, demand shorter build times, and require overtime labor costs. Corporate exhibitors may require special, brand-specific materials and high levels of fit and finish. The fabricator may bring in special craftspeople and master carpenters who earn a higher wage.

Corporate exhibits can be vast in size. As opposed to a simple booth, these exhibits can be two-story constructions set on a 900-square-foot base—bigger than some houses and requiring four thousand labor hours or more to build. After being approved by the client in the fabricator's warehouse, it will be disassembled and prepared for shipping, with instructions for a dedicated build team to take charge of installation and dismantling at the venue. After the show, a corporate exhibit is typically returned to the shop where it was built for storage and ongoing exhibit management.

Make sure freight labels and counts are accurate and that BOL forms are in place, acting as a receipt that materials have been picked up and/or delivered at a certain time and in good order. Whoever has the BOL has the materials.

In the whirlwind of executing a live event, meticulous planning and seamless execution are paramount. From orchestrating a smooth load-in process to providing white-glove service, every detail contributes to the success of the event. By implementing best practices and thinking on your feet, you can help ensure that everything runs like clockwork, exceeding expectations and solidifying your reputation for excellence.

PRO TIPS:

- Logistics management is an art and a science; some convention centers are introducing high-tech systems to facilitate load-in and load-out, but all processes must be adhered to.

- To facilitate exhibitor load-in efforts, have a dedicated team member stationed at entrances to direct vendors and exhibitors to their designated load-in areas. Exhibitors can avoid headaches (caused by weather and other disruptions) by having their materials shipped to the local staging warehouse in advance of load-in dates.

- Exhibitors do best when they think through the needs of their intended customers and deploy human/technology resources in a focused way.

- Agencies/GSCs should be proactive about supporting exhibitors, especially those who are new to event marketing.

- Offer premium add-on services to corporate clients, such as customized catering options or branded promotional materials to enhance the overall corporate event experience.

- Provide comprehensive post-event reporting and analysis to corporate event clients to demonstrate the impact and ROI of their investment in the event.

- Offer exclusive networking opportunities or VIP experiences to corporate event attendees on the day of the event to foster meaningful connections.

CHAPTER 16

Conducting the Event

TO-DO LIST:

- Conduct a final preview of the latest plan and give the team a chance to weigh in on minor tweaks and details.

- Double-check arrangements with all vendors, from caterers to technology providers, ensuring they are clear on their roles and timings.

- Document any changes made to the original design or plan.

- Conduct a final check-in with the team, and conduct a walk-through prior to launching the show. Confirm safety protocols are in place.

- Reassess the emergency and contingency plans with the team, ensuring everyone knows the protocols for various scenarios.

- Double-check contracts and arrangements with all vendors, from caterers to technology providers, ensuring they are clear on their roles and timings.

- Reassess the safety, emergency, and contingency plans with the team, ensuring everyone knows the protocols for various scenarios.

- Confirm security arrangements, access-control measures, and any required safety inspections.

continued

- Confirm arrangements for guest transport, parking logistics, and any special accommodations for VIP attendees.

- Go through the budget one last time to ensure all expenses are accounted for and within the allocated budget.

- Compile a comprehensive day-of-event checklist for team leaders, ensuring nothing is overlooked during the event.

- Once the event is underway, schedule daily huddles to manage each activity as it unfolds and adjust as opportunities arise.

- Share all revised documentation with the team and get approval from the decision-makers and key team members.

- Commence load-out activities, being mindful of timeline and sustainability commitments.

ALMOST SHOW TIME

The final walk-through is something of a tradition, an opportunity to take a last look, tweak, and clean up from any last-minute activity. Adrenaline is high, which is good, because exhaustion is also a factor this close to opening the doors. Mind your wellness, check that safety protocols are being followed, and be kind to each other.

Prepare for the fire marshal, who will typically inspect your event the day before it opens. The plans you submitted at least twenty days before the show opens may not have been approved yet, depending on the fire marshal's workload. The event manager often accompanies the fire marshal, along with the account lead, executive producer, and technical director. Be prepared with your latest CAD drawings, required certification, and any other relevant materials. Have resources necessary to make any last-minute adjustments that the fire marshal requires.

A creative director or production designer will walk the show before the doors open in case any polishing or refinement is in order. Other members of the event team should walk through the event when it's underway, observing real people interacting with exhibits and activities, to audit how well things are working and to make any notes that will inform the debrief session scheduled for after the show closes.

When you're walking through a show, make a note of the many things you should watch for. Each member of the team will have their own priorities, but be sure to take the opportunity to experience how the flow of traffic feels, see if site lines and signage work as expected, and listen to what exhibitors and attendees are talking about. When the strategist walks the show, they can observe how things are playing out in real time and think about any course corrections they'd like to implement right away, recommendations going forward, or ideas to consider in the next event cycle.

If possible, everyone on the team should walk the floor and think about the top three objectives outlined when the event was in the earliest planning stages, asking how they play out in reality, taking notes, and sharing them as appropriate. Before the doors open, have a plan to confirm that any adjustments have been documented and approved, that all affected parties have been informed, and that everyone is good to go.

ONGOING COMMUNICATION

Once an event kicks off, make an effort to huddle each morning to ensure you're all on the same page. Anything can happen, and you can't plan for every remote contingency when infinite variables are in play, but most potential problems can be preempted by continuous, clear communication. If anyone sees a potential problem, have them bring it up in the morning huddle, when it can be quickly analyzed, rather than waiting and risking disrupting activities that are already underway. Quick checklists of the day's activities can help team members double-check that required arrangements are in place. The morning huddle is also a good time to check on potential external disruptors—weather that could interfere with attendance or delay guest speakers, breaking news that could distract audiences, or health and safety concerns that could be preempted with a quick response.

ON-SITE DOCUMENTATION

With the event underway, make sure everyone takes notes and photos to help document the experience. This information captures a clear picture of what really happens at an event, with real human beings filling the space, finding the best route through the exposition area, and spending time at their favorite networking space.

To make sure this is fruitful, it may help to be intentional about your approach to on-site documentation, so explicitly ask team members to make this part of the process. Ask people to think about how different user groups are experiencing the event. Revisit any big decisions the team made that could be checked or validated on a walk-through. Did you guess right, or should something be refined during the next show cycle? On-site documentation is vital to capturing project implementation results and insights so the team can learn from successes and mistakes. Note any observations that should be shared in the debrief session.

Try these tactics to organize your team before they conduct their walk-throughs.

- Designate one or more team members to capture and categorize all of the information as it comes in. Be explicit in how and when to deliver these notes, photos, videos, and even attendee interviews. For example, if you want materials loaded to the online platform that's been used throughout the event, create a folder for on-site documentation with subfolders for notes and other media. Ask people to update in real time, if possible, or at least ask to have things uploaded by a specific date.

- Remind the team to be objective when recording their observations. It's important to document what works and what falls short of expectations. It's not about blaming an individual or team, but about opportunities for improvement.

- If the event covers multiple venues and experiences, assign people to cover each, so there are no gaps in your documentation.

- Capture as much detail as possible using photos. Is there a fit and finish problem, an attendee expressing delight at a surprising event moment, a special effect in the general session that drew gasps? Let's see it.

- Consider other ways to capture data that will help create a clearer picture of challenges and opportunities. Use a floor plan and highlight any pinch points. What do security cameras, NFC data, or beacons reveal about traffic patterns? Chat with participants at lunch and during networking opportunities to see what they think about the food, the venues, the hospitality, and everything that should contribute to a memorable experience.

- Ask everyone to follow these minimal steps: 1) Grab your phone or a camera and notebook; 2) Walk the space, documenting as you go; 3) Capture the essential experience; 4) Look for things you were expecting and note them for later; and 5) Share your findings with the team by uploading them or presenting them to the team in a formal debrief session.

PRODUCING THE EVENT

Event managers often perform hosting functions for the event and may be called on to act as a tour guide for VIPs, special guests, and sponsors. They will have press interviews to organize and may make presentations onstage for awards or introductions. Tight communication is critical when a show is underway; cell phones work but two-way radios ensure immediate, discreet, reliable communication between core production team members. Follow an established protocol regarding which channels (frequencies) to use under which circumstances, whether earphones are required (to avoid audio spillover), and when and where radios should be recharged.

THE PRODUCTION OFFICE

Any event may have two or three production offices, with one for the event manager's team, one for the agency/GSC, and others as needed if there is a hospitality/travel partner. Don't try to combine offices—it's not productive. The event manager staff needs a dedicated place to act as their on-site office and will require privacy to discuss confidential business, take care of executive requests, and huddle as needed. The agency's production office will have banks of computers for writers, AV support, producers, designers, and crew, plus charging stations and boxes full of agendas, giveaways, props, decor, and other things used to produce the show. It's a good idea to keep an emergency kit on hand, including basic first aid supplies, spare batteries, and backup phone chargers, to swiftly address any unexpected issues during the event.

THE ON-SITE PRODUCTION SCHEDULE

The on-site production schedule can be a simple Excel spreadsheet or table that begins with the first travel day for the lead crew entering the venue and has an hour-by-hour entry for what needs to happen, where it needs to happen, and who needs to do it. Each day of the event has its own section, with the last entry indicating that load-out is complete, power has been disconnected, any special equipment has been picked up for return, and all crew members have checked out and are traveling home or to the next venue.

THE GENERAL SESSION

These sessions often showcase company executives, presenting sponsors, celebrity-level guest speakers, product announcements, and other media-worthy events. Include time for a tech rehearsal (conducted without presenters) to dial in AV settings and cues. This helps ensure a smooth dress rehearsal with presenters—ideally a straight run-through—where everyone can focus on finessing their part of the show and checking overall presentation lengths. Hopefully, any executive presenters will have already rehearsed off-site so that they can use their time onstage to practice interacting with show elements and choreographing movement as appropriate. If any presenters need more rehearsal, arrange to have a small breakout room set up on-site, so they can practice with the full teleprompter setup, AV monitors, and crew. Because they have other demands on their time, you may need to schedule these rehearsals at odd hours of the day; coordinate with administrative assistants to confirm availability.

THE SHOW CALLER/STAGE MANAGER CALLS THE SHOTS

When rehearsals and the actual general session are underway, the show caller—often referred to as the *stage manager*—is in charge. Some events use both a show caller and a stage manager, with the latter literally focused on coordinating stage action. They work out the choreography of stage action and work with the scenic, lighting, and audio designers the way a conductor works with an orchestra, bringing all the pieces together.

The show caller often sits in the back of the house (behind the audience) on a raised deck with the lighting designer and the audio engineer. They literally call each separate cue for the show, working from some combination of a script book, a run-of-show document, and monitors that have a live feed from the teleprompter, speaker-support visuals, and all video elements. Everyone on the crew is on headsets and takes direction from the show caller.

Between tight cues, the show caller may ask crew members to check for audio balance if ambient noise is an issue, to check focus if the image looks soft, to warn catering if the show is running late or early, and to make sure all presenters are in place with working microphones. If something unexpected happens, the show caller tells the crew how to respond and, as necessary, has a live house microphone to encourage the audience to stay seated or, as needed, to remain calm and evacuate the building.

PRODUCING FOR A LIVE VIRTUAL/ HYBRID AUDIENCE

The live events industry has embraced a hybrid, integrated approach, as the advantages of having a virtual extension in place for all live events are clear. More people can participate, including those who want to attend an event in person but are prohibited by obstacles ranging from too many demands on their time to health issues. Attendees appreciate the flexibility of being able to participate in the aspects of an event that are most relevant to their needs.

Offering virtual or hybrid options broadens your event's reach and helps exhibitors and sponsors tap into remote audiences. While it's natural to use the in-person live event as the hub for virtual offerings, it's essential to specifically design, produce, and deliver your content in a way that leverages the strength of streaming video formats. Think about your virtual show as a separate production, with dedicated staff managing their own specific budget and timeline.

Curate content that will be especially valuable to those participating remotely and offer it exclusively to them. It could be exhibitor webinars, virtual product showcases, or an online exhibitor directory where downloadable information is collected in an easy-to-find location, complete with special offers and opportunities to arrange private video conference sessions.

CREATE COMMUNITY

A key to making hybrid offerings work is to telegraph some of the live event excitement to the virtual audience in a meaningful way. Help remote viewers understand when and where they want to check in with you by posting a schedule of live streamed events. Create an exclusive virtual studio, with professional MCs who can provide context on everything shared and interview guest speakers before or after their presentations. Stay flexible—if something interesting or newsworthy happens at your event, create a special preview just for your virtual audience. Make them feel appreciated and glad they chose to participate.

Create community with technology solutions that connect participants in valuable ways. Create exclusive live chat opportunities with presenters that are only available to the virtual audience. Offer online meetups that allow for networking, discussion, meetings with exhibitors, and even product demonstrations. Maintain a live social stream, so fellow attendees can comment and share insights. Set up a virtual marketplace where exhibitors can connect with virtual audiences and sell their products and services on-site. Use AI to pair up interested virtual attendees for one-on-one chats. Leverage trends that work more easily online. Your virtual event can provide a framework to showcase user-generated content. Perhaps it's a collaborative framework, or something that allows voting up or down to raise money for scholarships or charity. Make it meaningful, and it will be worth your while.

Build out an exclusive virtual experience, and you'll be able to expand sponsorships and extend your digital offerings in ways that increase revenue potential and add value for all your event stakeholders.

MOVE-OUT

While some team members are making sure everything is running according to plan, others will be confirming that all necessary arrangements are in place to load out the show. Logistic planning is key, as everything needs to happen in a minimal amount of time. Another event is typically waiting to load in, and deadlines are absolute.

The account lead for the agency/GSC will schedule a move-out meeting to align all the teams before the event wraps up. The move-out generally looks like the load-in but run in reverse and at a faster speed. These critical hours create a final sense of how successfully the event was managed. Although production work may not seem as glamorous coming down as going up, event professionals know there's no time for wasted motion and no margin for error—the exact time everything must be out of the venue is etched in stone. Safety is still the top priority.

Bringing all the parties together allows everyone to coordinate efforts and deal with any challenges or opportunities. The high-minded goals that launched the event should be carried through to the final exit from the venue. For example, if an exhibitor isn't taking valuable materials, giveaways, food, or even floral decorations, identify a nearby cause-related organization to benefit from these donations.

Keep the flow of communication strong between everyone working the event. Depending on the scope of the event, the details of the move-out will vary. A typical agenda for a move-out meeting will cover the following:

- Freight doors and security schedule—the earliest time these doors can be safely opened

- Move-out bulletin (if applicable)

- Any areas of the show breaking early or late (for example, sessions that close before the exhibition area and can be struck first)

- The earliest time dismantling can start for each area (lobbies, meeting rooms, exhibit hall, etc.)

- The schedule for removing aisle carpeting (if applicable)

- The schedule for returning empty containers to each exhibit, so they can be dismantled and packed

- Areas that the venue/facility needs to clear at the close of the show (reception tables, etc.) to facilitate the rest of the move-out

- The dock schedule (the precise time trucks are scheduled for picking up loads at each dock)

- The facility schedule (i.e., when everything must officially be loaded out of each space within the venue)

- The freight elevator schedule—aligned with the dock schedule, as needed, so that all crates and containers can get where they need to be on time

- Sustainability considerations, including any items the customer is recycling, saving, or donating

- Items being shipped

- Items being stored

- Show management outbound shipment (if applicable)

- Labor crew calls and schedules

- Freight shipping and tracking schedules

- Post-show facility walk-through to confirm that everything is taken care of

PRO TIPS:

- Substitutions and changes to the plan are part of a healthy process, but always consult with the team leads and build experts first.

- It's easy to burn out your people—tag team as necessary to make sure everyone gets some downtime; respect union workers and all contracts.

- Stay on top of change requests that need to be reviewed and authorized for billing purposes.

- Iteration is key to the design process. Once a creative concept has been approved there is still room for improvement; give the build team (fabricators, riggers, AV, etc.) time to evaluate your plan and suggest practical improvements.

- As the event plan moves through logical stages of development, expect different teams to assume a leadership role, shifting from strategy to design to fabrication and logistics to production.

- A thorough workflow requires multiple steps for revision and approval; don't take shortcuts.

- When raising build problems with the team or with clients, present the problem with a choice of solutions.

- Set up your online communication platform with folders/document templates, etc., so that everyone on-site knows where to upload photos, videos, change-of-scope documentation, etc., to document this stage of the journey.

- For all formal presentations (general session, etc.), in order to make the most of limited onstage rehearsal time, consider adding teleprompter rehearsals in an off-line space prior so that all edits to the presentation have been incorporated before dress rehearsals.

- Details, details, details. Manage everything as tightly as possible so that there is room to grapple with the unexpected.

- Make every effort to have those who were involved in early stages of the event plan (especially the strategist) attend the event so they can audit what's working, what isn't, and make recommendations for improvement.

- Plan to support/enforce sustainability measures on-site; it's essential, no longer a "nice to have."

- Including representatives from the host city, venue/convention center, and local community/businesses in your planning and communications process should be standard operating procedure.

- As soon as possible in your process, establish a clear line of communication for all on-site crew and team leads (using apps, email, online platforms, shortwave radios, etc.) so that it's in place before it becomes a critical need.

- Live events are stressful. Watch each other's backs and be kind. Be prepared for the unexpected. Stay calm and focused and communicate clearly.

- When it comes to conversations between department leads, there's no such thing as overcommunication. Staying in constant contact is vital to the success of the plan. Ensure participation and insist on a process that supports full transparency.

- In phase 4, the event team will review the collaborative feedback document; build that out early (place labeled folder in the online space the team has been using all along), and set the expectation that team members should capture and upload key learnings as they happen. This will ensure that items don't fall through the cracks but are recorded as part of the continuous improvement process.

- Because so many live events include streaming video, it is good practice to record dress rehearsals. This can be used as archival content but also provides a backup if there are any technical disruptions to the broadcast.

REVIEW AND IMPROVE

- Review your original objectives, and ask everyone to evaluate how close you came to meeting them. Create a report summarizing key findings on metrics aligned with the original stated objectives and consider how well the event measured up.

- Ask yourselves: How will we do it better in the future? How can we leverage the knowledge gained from this event to improve the next one?

- Assign someone to begin preassembly of all results, photos, testimonials, data, social media posts, comments, videos, etc., in one final easy-to-find place (most likely in the file-sharing platform used throughout the event) that everyone can access.

- Send out a preliminary survey or feedback form to event team members, so they can capture insights while their memories are fresh.

- Reconvene the team to share findings and project outcomes, setting the stage for continuous improvement. Schedule this debrief session as soon after load-out as practical; ensure attendance by all team leads. Create an environment that encourages honest, improvement-focused feedback.

- Gain insights from project intelligence to improve work quality and efficiency and inform strategy, noting opportunities for improvement and celebrating wins.

- Note any issues or insights regarding safety, emergency, or risk-management and document them for future use.

- Celebrate your team effort and highlight significant wins.

- Gain interest—secure a commitment for the next event from team members (especially freelance/contract contributors).

In this fourth phase, your team reflects on the completed event, acknowledging accomplishments and mistakes, identifying opportunities for improvement in the next event cycle, and strengthening relationships between all stakeholders.

CHAPTER 17

Reflect on Performance

TO-DO LIST:

- Take time to conduct a full analysis after the event. A structured reflection will help identify areas of improvement and opportunities for growth in future events.

- Create a digital archive system with clear categorization for all event artifacts, such as photos, videos, and attendee feedback. This organized approach will streamline future event-planning processes and make it easier to reference past successes and challenges.

- Dive deeper into event analytics by analyzing attendee demographics, engagement patterns, and conversion rates. This granular understanding will help optimize future marketing strategies and tailor event experiences to better meet attendee preferences.

- Schedule follow-up meetings with stakeholders and team members to gather qualitative feedback on the event's execution and impact. Actively listening to their perspectives can uncover valuable insights and strengthen relationships for future collaborations.

- Analyze budget variances to uncover underlying trends and patterns in event spending. Understanding the story behind

continued

> the numbers will empower you to make more informed budgeting decisions for future events.
>
> • Keep a running document of lessons learned and actionable insights from each aspect of the event, including what you would change next time. This ongoing reflection will serve as a valuable resource for continuously improving event-planning processes and outcomes.
>
> • Leverage user-generated content from the event, such as attendee testimonials and social media posts, to fuel post-event marketing campaigns. Authentic content created by attendees can significantly enhance your marketing efforts and generate buzz for future events.

This final phase of the process is a critical step in the life of an event. Without vigilance, it can slip through the cracks if everyone heads off to work on the next event without sharing the insights they gained from this one.

Throughout each phase of the event cycle, we urge people to document what's happening, noting where revisions are required and tracking how victory was snatched from the jaws of defeat. This documentation isn't very useful if it's not collected, reviewed by all the players, and stored in a place where it can be readily accessed and looked at again when the next event kicks off.

You may want to hold a celebration at the end of the event, and that's fine, but the data you'll need to review as a team will take time to decipher and will require a dedicated debrief session. Set a date (not more than four weeks out) to reconvene the team for a mandatory debriefing session. Keep it celebratory but be clear that the agenda is designed to share what you've learned and invite input. This final meeting will probably include the client, boss, or decision-maker to whom you're accountable for the success of the event.

COLLECT AND SORT EVENT ARTIFACTS

Hopefully, your team designated someone to collect and organize all the photos, documents, change forms, surveys, metrics, and other data gathered throughout the event. Ideally, they're all now in folders on the team's shared drive, where various teammates have already been using this Cloud-based space to upload various artifacts themselves.

If your event drew publicity or social media posts, capture a relevant sampling of those as well. Any surveys conducted with discrete audiences or data gathered as part of the show (second screen, gaming events, heat maps and beacons to show traffic patterns, etc.) should be included.

It's important to make all documentation available to the team, but before you do, have the account lead, creative director, and/or members of their teams take a first stab at contextualizing everything. You don't have to wait for all of the data to come in to start reviewing and sorting. Stories quickly emerge about aspects of the event that captured attendees' imaginations or left them disappointed.

Prep for a debrief session by creating a presentation deck (PowerPoint/ Keynote) or some other form of designed document to be shared with the larger group. You may want to post this debrief document on a shared drive so that people can directly add their input, or you may prefer to present initial findings and then invite input you can edit. After you have feedback from the event team, present the debrief document to your "customers" (anyone invested in the outcome of the event).

REVISIT YOUR OBJECTIVES

Go back to your original definition of *beautiful* in the first phase of planning your event. It's time to revisit those top three objectives and

KPIs to evaluate your success. Take time to consider each objective independently, asking yourself whether the event measured up to your stated goals and examining the proof points, learnings, and wins associated with each. Some metrics will speak for themselves, especially hard numbers (attendance figures, revenue, or exhibit space that's already been booked for the following year). Other metrics are more challenging to analyze (qualitative post-event surveys, exit interviews, and social media posts). Most plans entail some level of mission creep between ideation and execution, which might be good, but be honest in calling it out.

As members of the team are whisked away to other assignments, make it as easy as possible for them to contribute feedback and insights about what worked and what didn't. Collect this input and make sure it's represented in the document you ultimately share with the team at the debrief session. Send your team leads a link to the debrief folder and request their input, encouraging them to share the preliminary findings with their team members as appropriate.

UNDERSTAND THE ANALYTICS

Data can be overwhelming. Think about what you're hoping to learn. Try to identify trends in the feedback that tell a story. For example, imagine you eliminated a legacy aspect of the event; what does the feedback tell you about that decision? Did anyone notice what was missing? Did the new features created with those funds delight your audience? Is it important to appease anyone who was unhappy? What are the demographics of the people who approved and disapproved, and which group is more important to the event's future?

You may uncover questions you don't have answers to. Sometimes post-event survey results raise issues the team was unaware of when the event was in progress. There may be different theories about how or why something unplanned occurred. These are all good reasons to conduct follow-up interviews of stakeholders inside and outside of your team to get their impression.

CONDUCTING FOLLOW-UP INTERVIEWS

Because each person working on an event is focused on their part of the experience, the insights gained from team interviews can be enlightening. It also gives team members a chance to give credit to anyone who contributed to their success and helps build empathy within the group that fought in the trenches together. If some aspect of the event fell short of expectations, team members who were at the scene are positioned to explain why and how things got off track. Ideally, these interviews can be conducted in person so you can speak face-to-face; video calls are an acceptable and perhaps more realistic option for geographically dispersed teams. Get different perspectives and be intentional about talking to diverse groups and disciplines, such as coworkers, SMEs, vendors, safety and risk-management teams, clients/approvers, or end users. Be sure to follow up while the event is still fresh in their minds.

Keep the interview conversational but structured, so you don't waste time. Identify the specific issues and topics you want to address and share a list of questions in advance; reference the team's original goals and objectives, so responses stay in the context of the event's success or failure. Invite team members to participate in the interview sessions if it makes sense. Ask to record the sessions and generate transcripts, so you can pull direct quotes. Look for common themes in the responses and use those quotes as part of the event documentation that you'll share with the group and store for posterity. These details could prove priceless when the team begins planning for the next event.

EVERY BUDGET TELLS A STORY

It may be a while before all departments on the team have submitted their invoices, but basic budget reconciliation should have been ongoing throughout the whole process. If everyone's done their job, the executive producer will know where the budget stands and where overages (hopefully approved) have occurred. With many events, the budget reconciliation process reveals information that needs to be shared with the team.

Most event production veterans use their own metrics, tools, and hacks to preempt disaster and avoid overages. These "canary in the coal mine" tricks (usually unique to their process) are effective early warning systems.

For example, a labor budget tool can be used to examine exhibitors submitting power requests during the week before the show; if there's a big discrepancy between a past show and the one ready to load in, the account supervisor will start calling people to see if there's been a mix-up and get to the bottom of the problem. Experienced scenic designers may double-check dimensions provided by the venue if they know the fit will be tight, especially if recent venue renovations might not be reflected in their published floor plans. A master carpenter looking at specs for a new exhibit will spot a problem with key design elements and suggest a correction long before materials are ordered. It's hard to document potential missteps that are corrected before they become a problem, but whenever possible, these should also be captured to inform the next event.

When costs come in well beyond the approved budget—whether items that should have been included were missed, things were estimated at an outdated or inaccurate price, or graphics were already in production when a change came through—most mistakes are the result of a communication error. Good people acting on bad information may end up doing the wrong thing. Budget discrepancies point to a serious gap in the process that must be fixed going forward. Ensure that your project management includes a way to flag potential challenges early, so they can be remedied in advance or on-site to avoid overages. Include steps to secure an authorized approval signature on changes that impact the budget.

Here are some examples of common hurdles to watch out for, so mistakes aren't repeated in the future.

- If someone with budget authority has approved an overage in one area because they know they can cover it with a contingency budget they have authority to use, that's fine. But make sure it's clearly recorded, so future estimates are more accurate and bad assumptions aren't passed along in future budgeting.

- When a budgeted line item represents a huge discount (negotiated as a result of a vendor's bid for future work, a onetime procurement allowance, items repurposed from a previous event, or some other anomaly), make sure the discount is documented, or someone preparing a future budget may think that's the going rate.

- If and when on-site additions occur, make sure they have been tracked, approved, and detailed in the budget. Additions are normal, but they reflect a change in scope and should be indicated, so they don't impact the original budget calculations and are called out for consideration in creating the budget for the next event.

- If an agency or GSC feels they don't need to report their own team's hours accurately, the next event can't be planned properly. For example, if the design team spent twice as many hours as were budgeted, the account lead may not reflect them in the invoice because they know they won't be billing for those hours anyway; but underreporting hours perpetuates a myth that the event can be designed in less time than is actually needed. Most people look at previous event budgets to estimate the number of billable hours to assign to new assignments. If actual hours aren't documented, the mistake will be repeated in the next event.

The agency and all vendors working on a job must exercise absolute integrity in submitting invoices that are accurate and based on the initially contracted agreement. This isn't just a question of ethical business practices; it's a road map for the next event. Submitting anything not perfectly transparent and accurate will inevitably form an inaccurate basis for next year's budget.

DOCUMENT WHAT YOU WOULD CHANGE

Share a document that contains actual budget numbers, revisions, and relevant metrics with the entire team in a final wrap-up session. Make thoughtful observations on the event's many success stories and note a few places to improve next time. Consider timing, budget, quality, and input from the team and decision-makers in your presentation.

POWERHOUSE STRATEGIES FOR MASTERING POST-EVENT MARKETING

After the venue clears out, it's time to think about post-event marketing. This pivotal phase, where the success of your event extends far beyond its physical presence, holds the potential to amplify your brand and cultivate lasting relationships. You've already gathered feedback and sent out comprehensive surveys to attendees to gain valuable insights into their event experience. You've conducted one-on-one interviews with key stakeholders to uncover nuanced feedback and suggestions for improvement. You've analyzed social media chatter and sentiment to gauge the overall reception of your event. Utilize these insights to unlock the full potential of your post-event marketing efforts.

- **Create compelling recap content:**
  - Develop visually captivating infographics that highlight key statistics, moments, and takeaways from the event.
  - Craft engaging blog posts that delve into the most impactful sessions, discussions, and presentations.

- Produce dynamic video recaps that capture the energy and essence of the event, driving nostalgia and engagement.

- **Cultivate testimonials and social proof:**

  - Reach out to attendees, speakers, and sponsors for authentic testimonials that showcase the value of your event.

  - Curate user-generated content (UGC) from social media platforms, amplifying positive experiences and interactions.

  - Showcase testimonials and UGC across your marketing channels to build trust and credibility with your audience.

- **Foster personalized follow-up engagement:**

  - Craft personalized follow-up emails that express gratitude, share valuable resources, and encourage further engagement.

  - Offer exclusive post-event discounts or promotions as a token of appreciation for attendees' participation.

  - Schedule one-on-one follow-up calls or meetings with key leads to deepen relationships and explore potential collaborations.

- **Maximize social media presence:**

  - Leverage social media platforms to share event highlights, behind-the-scenes moments, and attendee testimonials.

  - Engage with attendees and followers by responding to comments, questions, and messages promptly and authentically.

  - Run targeted social media ads to retarget event attendees and drive traffic to post-event content and resources.

More Tips:

- **Collect feedback:** Send out surveys to attendees to gather feedback on their experience.

- **Highlight key moments:** Share highlights from the event on social media and in email newsletters.

- **Create recap content:** Develop blog posts, videos, or infographics that summarize key takeaways from the event.

- **Share testimonials:** Feature testimonials from attendees, speakers, and sponsors to build credibility.

- **Send follow-up emails:** Send personalized follow-up emails to attendees, thanking them for participating and providing relevant resources.

- **Utilize user-generated content:** Repurpose photos, videos, and posts shared by attendees on social media to extend the event's reach.

- **Offer exclusive content:** Provide exclusive access to additional content or resources related to the event for attendees.

- **Host webinars or Q&A sessions:** Organize webinars or Q&A sessions with speakers to continue the conversation and engage with attendees.

- **Launch a post-event campaign:** Develop a targeted marketing campaign to promote related products, services, or upcoming events.

- **Create a landing page:** Build a dedicated landing page on your website to showcase post-event content and resources.

- **Partner with influencers:** Collaborate with influencers or industry experts to amplify your post-event marketing efforts.

- **Run retargeting ads:** Launch retargeting ads on social media or other platforms to reengage attendees and website visitors.

- **Offer discounts or promotions:** Provide special discounts or promotions on products or services featured at the event.

- **Host a virtual networking event:** Organize a virtual networking event for attendees to connect with each other and with your team.

- **Share behind-the-scenes content:** Offer a behind-the-scenes look at the event-planning process or share stories about memorable moments.

- **Publish case studies:** Create case studies highlighting successful outcomes or partnerships that originated from the event.

- **Optimize SEO:** Optimize your website and content for relevant keywords related to the event to attract organic traffic.

- **Engage with social media mentions:** Monitor social media mentions of the event and engage with users by responding to comments and messages.

- **Leverage email automation:** Set up automated email sequences to nurture leads and keep them engaged with your brand after the event.

- **Create interactive content:** Develop interactive content such as quizzes or polls related to the event theme or topics.

- **Offer on-demand content:** Make event recordings or presentations available on demand for those who couldn't attend live.

These tips should help you effectively leverage your post-event marketing strategies to maximize the impact of your event and continue engaging with attendees beyond the live experience.

Transform post-event marketing into a catalyst for sustained growth and engagement. From harnessing feedback to nurturing leads, each step propels your brand forward, solidifying its place in the hearts and minds of your audience.

Embrace the opportunity to extend the impact of your event, forging connections that endure long after the lights have dimmed and the crowds have dispersed.

PRO TIPS:

- **Provide resources for continued learning.** Share articles, white papers, or e-books that delve deeper into topics covered at the event.

- **Host a post-event AMA (ask me anything).** Invite attendees to submit questions for a post-event AMA session with key speakers or organizers.

- **Encourage referrals.** Implement a referral program where attendees can earn rewards for referring others to your products or services.

- **Measure and analyze results.** Track key metrics such as website traffic, email open rates, and sales to evaluate the success of your post-event marketing efforts and inform future strategies.

CHAPTER 18

Maximize Success through Post-Event Debriefing

TO-DO LIST:

- Be sure to highlight any wins as you review the results and reference the supporting data. Creating clarity around what worked and what didn't is the point of creating a debrief document to be shared after the event.

- Don't just upload the debrief document and walk away, even though the debrief document officially puts the whole assignment to bed. Think about who might benefit from this resource—the marketing team, public relations, training teams, etc.—and make sure they know where to find it.

- If there has been a breakthrough moment, a first-time use of technology or other design resources, consider creating a case study that can be easily shared.

THE DEBRIEF DOCUMENT

Months of meticulous planning and execution culminates in the live event itself. After the show, as attendees disperse, it's time for you to start building your debrief document. The debrief document helps bring clarity to the chaos that accompanies any live event. By dissecting what worked and what didn't with surgical precision, this document can serve as a beacon, guiding future endeavors toward even greater success.

The debrief document is a quest for clarity. Its comprehensive examination of every facet of the event, from conception through execution, meticulously dissects each component, giving you invaluable insights into the efficacy of your strategies and tactics and painting a vivid picture of the event's triumphs and challenges. Be sure to highlight the victories that were achieved, a testament to everyone's hard work as well as invaluable reference points for future endeavors.

The debrief document isn't an artifact to be filed away and forgotten. Instead, it's a resource with the power to shape future events. Ensure the document is easily accessible to relevant stakeholders, so its insights can be leveraged to inform and enrich future strategies.

The debrief document also serves as the proverbial final chapter in the saga of the live event. By encapsulating the entirety of the event, from its inception to its culmination, it officially puts the assignment to bed. More than a mere formality, this act of closure marks the beginning of a new chapter, one fueled by the insights and learnings gleaned from the debriefing process, helping ensure that each subsequent event is a success.

POST-EVENT ANALYSIS: THE BONES OF A DEBRIEF DOCUMENT

Some of the most valuable insights are gained during the post-event phase. The debrief document, a cornerstone of post-event analysis, serves as a comprehensive record of the event's successes, challenges, and lessons learned. The essential components of an exemplary debrief document provide actionable insights for future events.

- **Introduction and purpose:** At the outset of the debrief document, clarity on the purpose is crucial. It sets the tone for the entire analysis, emphasizing the importance of reflection and improvement. By articulating the purpose clearly, stakeholders understand the intent behind the document and are more likely to engage with its findings.

- **Event overview:** A thorough event overview lays the foundation for the rest of the debrief document. It encapsulates the event's objectives, target audience, and key stakeholders, providing context for the subsequent analysis. Including details on event components such as sessions, speakers, and activities helps stakeholders recall the event's scope and scale.

- **Key metrics and performance data:** Data-driven insights are the backbone of any effective debrief document. By analyzing key performance metrics, such as attendance numbers, engagement levels, and feedback ratings, organizers can gauge the event's success objectively. Visualizing data through charts, graphs, and tables enhances comprehension and facilitates trend identification.

- **Successes and achievements:** Celebrating successes and achievements is not only gratifying but also informative. By highlighting positive feedback, successful partnerships, or innovative features, organizers acknowledge what worked well and why. Understanding the factors that contributed to these successes enables organizers to replicate and build upon them in future events.

- **Challenges and lessons learned:** Equally important as celebrating successes is acknowledging challenges and lessons learned. Identifying root causes, discussing mitigation strategies, and extracting key insights are essential for continuous improvement. Transparently addressing challenges demonstrates a commitment to growth and resilience in the face of adversity.

- **Technology and design innovations:** Innovation often distinguishes exceptional events from mediocre ones. Documenting breakthrough moments or innovative use of technology/design resources provides valuable insights into what captivated attendees and enhanced their experience. Detailed case studies illustrate the effectiveness and impact of these innovations, inspiring future creativity.

- **Recommendations for future events:** The true value of a debrief document lies in its ability to inform future event-planning efforts. Actionable recommendations derived from insights gained enable organizers to iterate and improve continually. Whether it's optimizing logistics, enhancing content delivery, or refining audience engagement strategies, recommendations guide future decision-making.

- **Conclusion and next steps:** In the conclusion, summarizing key findings and outlining next steps is essential for closure and clarity. By distilling insights into actionable takeaways, organizers ensure that the debriefing process translates into tangible improvements. Encouraging ongoing reflection and continuous improvement fosters a culture of excellence in event-planning practices.

- **Appendixes:** Supplementing the debrief document with appendixes, such as survey results, feedback summaries, or case studies, provides additional context and depth. These supporting materials validate findings and offer stakeholders a more comprehensive understanding of the event's impact.

A well-crafted debrief document is more than a useful post-event formality. It's a road map for future success. By leveraging insights gleaned from reflection and analysis, you can continuously elevate the attendee experience and deliver exceptional events time after time.

THE DEBRIEF SESSION

Discuss the debrief document with the team in a post-event session. If the budget and timeline were met, prioritize this debrief session to focus on how well other objectives were met; but if the budget or timeline had issues, be sure to spell that out in the debrief document, and address it in the debrief session.

Make sure this final team session—and the presentation deck you share with the team—is meaningful. The account lead, executive producer, and strategist should present the material and invite feedback from the team, with the debrief document working as an agenda to keep things purposeful and on track.

Set aside time within a month after the event, so the team can all participate in a debrief session. It's important to provide an opportunity to discuss the event feedback that's been gathered and also to understand the timeline and budget implications.

Begin by anchoring the review in the key takeaways. Remind everyone of the original top three objectives you started with, the key challenges you faced at the onset of the process, and any insights that shaped the plan you ended up using. Go through each objective, one at a time, and show examples of how that objective was met. Use photos and videos but also be sure to include actual metrics. Include quotes from attendees, clients, exhibitors, sponsors, and the media. For each objective, make a list of what worked and what could have worked better. Did you achieve what you intended? What are the nuances? What are the insights?

Show inspiring photos and video clips from the actual event to recapture the *esprit de corps* and rekindle impressions that made the event special. Try to represent as many key areas as you can to help ensure that everyone's work is appreciated. Thank everyone for their contributions, share fun facts, call out the great saves, describe superhuman efforts, and remember hilarious shared moments.

In-person sessions are best, but not always possible. If this session is hybrid or hosted on a virtual platform, make sure the functionality promotes interaction (live chat, voting, quick surveys). In addition to identifying a moderator for the session and key presenters, be sure someone is assigned to take notes. And don't forget to record the session so that it can be shared and reviewed later, especially as there will always be some who cannot attend.

Make clear, explicit statements that summarize everything you've gathered in the context of the objectives. For example, "Although we chose to limit the number of exhibitors this year to reduce congestion on the trade show floor, we raised the cost of exhibit space and increased revenues, supplemented by sponsor engagement strategies. Post-event surveys indicate that exhibitors gave the event high marks, and we've already sold 80 percent of the space for next year's show. Attendees appreciated that the show floor felt more open than in the past."

Be clear about where to improve and be sure to reference data points that support course correction. Carefully review any specific learnings from the budget reconciliation process. Consider adjusting any steps in the process that could improve results next time, including timelines, budget, and the satisfaction of each stakeholder group.

CELEBRATE THE OPPORTUNITY TO IMPROVE

No one enjoys getting advice; harsh criticism is even worse. That said, people who care can help us be better people by offering constructive feedback. Establish from the outset that the team has an obligation to question and challenge decisions and results. Remind them that constructive feedback is part of the process of continuous improvement. Work to foster candid discussion and prevent ill will.

- Establish a safe place to hold this session. Opt for neutral ground, where no one has a home court advantage. Step out of the office so people aren't interrupted by other business, but choose a sufficiently private space where confidential discussions won't be overheard.

- Begin the discussion on an upbeat note and celebrate successes. It builds teamwork and motivates people to do a better job when they see that extra efforts are noticed. Sharing a few kind words about the team's accomplishments can be good for everyone's sense of well-being.

- Invite people to discuss areas for improvement. Invite each member of the team to discuss their insights and learnings, both positive and negative. Make sure the discussion stays healthy; if things threaten to become personal, take it offline.

- Take notes on the insights shared by team members and save them as documentation for future reference. Make sure all relevant insights are easily accessible to anyone who might need them in the future.

DATA VISUALIZATION TOOLS TO ENHANCE POST-EVENT ANALYSIS

Data visualization tools can reveal invaluable insights into event activities, attendee engagement, and key metrics. Events that utilize live, real-time visualization tools can track attendee behavior, session popularity, and interaction levels as the event unfolds. While this immediate feedback can enable prompt adjustments and optimization strategies during the event itself, it may be even more valuable in the debrief session. A key to continuous improvement is understanding and documenting the results, and the right data visualization tools can help.

- **Trend identification:** These tools help in identifying and understanding trends that emerge during the event. By aggregating data from various sources, such as attendee surveys, social media interactions, and session attendance, visualization tools can highlight patterns and tendencies. This facilitates the identification of popular topics, preferred engagement formats, and areas for improvement. Composite visuals generated by data visualization tools play a crucial role in identifying and addressing important trends. These composites offer a comprehensive view of various data points, empowering the team to recognize patterns and adapt strategies for enhanced event outcomes.

- **Persona profiling:** Data visualization tools aid in creating detailed attendee personas post event. By analyzing demographic data, session preferences, and interaction patterns, teams can segment attendees into distinct groups. Visual representations of these personas help in understanding their needs, interests, and behavior, enabling personalized follow-up strategies. By providing a real-time graphic snapshot, these tools help you better understand your audience, enabling more targeted marketing strategies for future events.

- **Performance evaluation:** Post-event analysis becomes more effective with visualization tools by providing a comprehensive overview of event performance. Through interactive dashboards, teams can assess the success of different sessions, speakers, and activities based on attendance rates, feedback scores, and engagement metrics. This holistic evaluation guides future event planning and content curation decisions.

- **Strategic decision-making:** Visualization tools empower teams to make informed strategic decisions based on actionable insights derived from event data. By visualizing KPIs and comparative metrics, stakeholders can identify strengths, weaknesses, and opportunities for growth. This data-driven approach ensures that post-event debriefings are focused on actionable strategies and improvements.

- **Actionable analytics:** While visualization tools provide a snapshot of data, their true power lies in facilitating deep, actionable analysis. By asking pertinent questions and strategically analyzing the data, event organizers can derive meaningful insights that drive future decision-making and improvements.

- **Strategic customization:** Although visualization tools offer a broad overview, thorough and individualized customization requires a strategic approach to data analysis. These tools act as a starting point, guiding teams to ask the right questions and delve into specific data points that align with their strategic goals.

- **Enhancing debriefing sessions:** Post-event debriefing sessions are significantly enhanced with data visualization tools. These tools aid in summarizing complex datasets into digestible visuals, making it easier for teams to review and discuss the event's performance and identify areas for refinement.

- **Facilitating collaboration:** Visualization tools become common ground for teams, facilitating collaboration during debriefing sessions. The visual representation of data ensures that all team members, regardless of their technical expertise, can actively participate in discussions and contribute valuable insights.

- **Driving continuous improvement:** The insights gained from data visualization tools become a foundation for continuous improvement. By understanding what worked well and what needs enhancement, event organizers can iteratively refine their strategies, ensuring each subsequent event becomes more successful than the last.

Data visualization tools play a crucial role in enhancing post-event analysis. By harnessing the power of visual representations, teams can derive actionable insights from event data to optimize future events, enhance attendee experiences, and foster a culture of continuous improvement in the events landscape.

NEXT STEPS CHECKLIST

Be clear with the team about what happens next and when it needs to happen. As the team looks ahead, members must imagine what's possible for the next event cycle. In many organizations, the same core team, with some substitutions, will tackle the next event; work could begin almost immediately.

- **Clarify immediate actions:** Clearly outline what needs to happen next and establish timelines for each action item.

- **Envision future event cycles:** Encourage the team to visualize and discuss possibilities for upcoming event cycles. Consider maintaining the core team structure with necessary substitutions.

- **Prompt initiation of work:** Emphasize the potential for immediate commencement of work for the next event. Highlight the importance of swift action to maintain momentum.

- **Foster effective workflow:** Promote a collaborative workflow that facilitates the delivery of exceptional attendee experiences. Emphasize the significance of improved internal communication channels.

- **Utilize shared tools for innovation:** Advocate for the utilization of shared tools that facilitate innovative solutions. Encourage the exploration of new technologies or methodologies to enhance event execution.

- **Drive cost savings and value addition:** Stress the importance of optimizing costs while adding value to event experiences. Explore strategies to achieve cost efficiency without compromising quality.

- **Empower attendees to make a difference:** Remind the team that successful event execution enables attendees to positively impact the world. Emphasize the broader purpose and impact of their work in facilitating meaningful connections and experiences.

Support your team as they effectively transition from the post-event phase to planning and executing the next event cycle, ensuring continued success and meaningful impact. If you do your work well, you enable the people who attend your events to change the world for the better.

PRO TIPS:

- When compiling your debrief document, include time stamps for all feedback and observations to provide context and aid in future analysis. Time stamps will streamline the review process during the debrief session and help pinpoint specific moments for improvement.

- During the debrief session, focus on actionable insights and avoid dwelling on issues that cannot be changed. Encourage open communication and brainstorming for innovative solutions to enhance future events.

- Use the debrief session not just to identify areas for improvement, but also to celebrate successes and milestones achieved during the event. Recognizing achievements boosts team morale and encourages continued dedication to excellence.

- Utilize data visualization tools like charts, graphs, and heat maps to transform raw event data into easily understandable insights.

Visual representations help pinpoint trends, patterns, and outliers for more informed decision-making.

- Create a next-steps checklist immediately after the debrief session to outline actionable tasks and responsibilities for implementing feedback and improvements. Prioritize tasks based on urgency and impact to ensure continuous progress and growth.

CHAPTER 19

Wrapping Up the Event

TO-DO LIST:

- Send personalized follow-up emails to speakers and presenters, expressing gratitude for their valuable contributions and sharing positive feedback from attendees.

- Handwrite thank-you cards to vendors and suppliers, expressing appreciation for their hard work and dedication to the event's success.

- Create and share a one-page post-event report outlining key metrics, attendee feedback, and lessons learned to inform future event strategies.

- Stay adaptable and resilient in the face of challenges, maintaining a positive attitude and focusing on solutions rather than obstacles.

I t's time to reflect, celebrate, and draw inspiration from your journey. From the initial brainstorming sessions to the final applause, each step has been a testament to your team's collective creativity, dedication, and unwavering commitment to excellence.

Pause to acknowledge the countless hours of hard work, the moments of ingenuity, and the bonds forged through collaboration. Your success is not merely measured by numbers on a balance sheet, but by the lasting impact you've made on everyone who has been part of this extraordinary journey.

Every great event begins with a clear, compelling vision that sets the stage for success. From conceptualization to execution, maintaining alignment with this vision ensures coherence and resonance throughout every aspect of the event. Create meaningful experiences that leave a lasting impression. Through impeccable execution, every element must come together harmoniously to create a seamless, immersive experience for all involved.

Foster a culture of adaptability and resilience to empower your team to overcome obstacles with creativity and grace, turning setbacks into opportunities for innovation. Strive for excellence in everything you do, from the smallest details to the grandest gestures. By setting high standards and holding yourselves accountable to them, you'll ensure that every event you touch is a success.

PRO TIPS:

- Make sure your budget includes time for contract or freelance professionals performing key roles on the team to participate in the debrief session. Their input could prove invaluable for making improvements in the next event cycle. Make it clear in your contract with them that they are expected to participate in the debrief session and will be compensated accordingly.

- Don't underestimate the power of reflection in your wrap-up process; it's not just about tying loose ends but also about distilling key learnings and insights to inform future endeavors. Consider incorporating a symbolic ritual or gesture during the wrap-up to mark the occasion and create a sense of closure and accomplishment.

CHAPTER 20

Conclusions and Beginnings

ACHIEVING EXCELLENCE AS AN EVENT PROFESSIONAL

Finding career success in event planning or live event management requires creativity, organization, and innovation. It is a fulfilling choice, whether you are just starting out, are looking to hone your expertise within the events arena, or have experience in another line of business but are ready to make a change. To thrive in this dynamic industry, event professionals must equip themselves with a repertoire of skills and strategies. Here are a few practical steps to advance your journey to becoming a masterful event professional.

- **Gain experience:**
  - Seek internships or entry-level positions in event-planning firms, venues, or organizations.
  - Volunteer for local events or assist friends and family with event coordination to gain hands-on experience.
  - Attend workshops, seminars, and conferences to immerse yourself in the world of event planning.

- **Develop organizational excellence:**

  - Master time management techniques to juggle multiple tasks and deadlines effectively.

  - Create detailed event timelines and checklists to stay organized and on track.

  - Utilize project management tools and software to streamline workflows and collaboration.

  - Stay informed about local regulations and permit requirements, understanding that each venue is unique.

- **Cultivate strong communication skills:**

  - Hone your ability to articulate ideas and listen actively to clients' needs and preferences.

  - Foster clear and concise communication with vendors, team members, and stakeholders.

  - Practice delegating tasks with grace and efficiency to foster collaboration.

  - Practice diplomacy and conflict resolution to navigate challenging situations with professionalism.

- **Stay ahead of trends and technologies:**

  - Stay abreast of emerging trends in event design, technology, and entertainment.

  - Embrace digital tools and event management software to enhance productivity and efficiency.

  - Innovate and adapt traditional event elements to meet the evolving preferences of clients and attendees.

- **Prioritize client satisfaction:**

  - Build rapport and trust with clients by understanding their vision and exceeding their expectations.

  - Provide personalized and attentive service throughout the event-planning process.

  - Solicit feedback and testimonials to continuously refine and improve your services.

- **Showcase your creativity:**

  - Develop a distinctive style and aesthetic that sets your events apart from the rest.

  - Incorporate unique elements and experiential activations to delight and engage attendees.

  - Collaborate with talented vendors and artisans to bring your creative vision to life.

- **Invest in continuing education:**

  - Pursue certifications or specialized training programs in event planning and management.

  - Attend workshops, webinars, and industry conferences to expand your knowledge and skills.

  - Stay curious and open-minded, embracing lifelong learning as a cornerstone of your professional development.

- **Foster strategic partnerships:**

  - Cultivate relationships with reliable and reputable vendors, venues, and service providers.

  - Collaborate with complementary businesses and organizations to expand your network and reach.

- Leverage partnerships to negotiate favorable terms and enhance the quality and diversity of your offerings.
- Network relentlessly within the industry to gain insider knowledge, opportunities, and mentorship. Personal connections can often open doors that traditional avenues cannot.

- Embrace flexibility and adaptability:
  - Anticipate and prepare for unforeseen challenges and changes in event logistics, weather, or other circumstances.
  - Maintain a calm and composed demeanor under pressure, leading your team with confidence and agility.
  - Embrace innovation and experimentation, embracing change as an opportunity for growth and improvement.

- Build a stellar reputation:
  - Uphold high standards of professionalism, integrity, and ethical conduct in all your interactions.
  - Deliver consistently exceptional experiences that earn rave reviews and referrals from satisfied clients.
  - Cultivate a strong online presence and reputation through social media, testimonials, and industry recognition.

Final Insights

Inside Live Events covers a lot of tactical, how-to information. As you design and execute your own event plan, keep in mind the higher purpose that drives your actions. Here are some high-level insights that can help you make your planned event the best it can be:

- Craft story-laden environments. Design environments that tell a story on their own, adding layers to the narrative and allowing participants to discover new elements as the experience unfolds.

- Mindfully use technology. Embrace technology as an enhancer, not a distraction. Leverage cutting-edge tools judiciously to complement the narrative without overshadowing the core experience.

- Implement interactive elements that encourage audience engagement, fostering a sense of cocreation and personal investment in the experience.

- Master the art of temporal pacing—know when to slow down for contemplation, when to build tension, and when to deliver exhilarating moments for maximum impact. Sculpt emotional peaks and valleys.

- Curate multisensory culminations. Elevate climactic moments by orchestrating a convergence of multiple senses, creating an unforgettable crescendo.

- Use the psychology of color and lighting to affect mood and perception, influencing how participants interpret and remember different aspects of the experience.

- Design experiences that can adapt dynamically to the environment, providing a personalized journey that responds to the unique context of each participant.

- Extend the narrative beyond the live event, creating an ongoing story arc that keeps participants engaged and invested in the experience long after it concludes.

- Intentionally introduce elements of cognitive dissonance to challenge perceptions, fostering deeper reflection and personal growth.

- Incorporate nostalgia thoughtfully. Use nostalgic elements sparingly and thoughtfully to evoke emotions and create a sense of connection between the past, present, and future.

- Recognize the power of silence as a design element, strategically incorporating moments of quiet to amplify the impact of subsequent sounds or visuals.

- Prioritize attendee engagement and interaction at every stage of the event design process; creating memorable experiences often hinges on fostering genuine connections and participation. Leverage technology creatively to enhance the live experience without overshadowing the human element; it should complement, not dominate, the event.

- Challenge conventional thinking and strive for innovative approaches that provoke thought and evoke emotion among attendees; memorable events often leave a lasting impact by daring to be different. Foster meaningful connections by curating opportunities for authentic interaction and dialogue, enabling participants to engage deeply with each other and the content.

- Delve into the psychology of memory formation to craft experiences that resonate long after the event concludes; consider sensory stimuli, emotional triggers, and storytelling techniques to imprint lasting memories. Pay meticulous attention to detail in all aspects of event design, from aesthetics to ambiance, as each element contributes to the overall memory-making process.

- Approach event planning with the mindset of a storyteller, crafting a cohesive narrative arc that guides attendees through a journey of discovery, transformation, or revelation. Seamlessly integrate key messages, themes, and experiences into the narrative to ensure a memorable and impactful event that resonates with participants on a deeper level.

- Analyze wins and seek to understand failures. Document key learnings. Debrief as a team and take time to celebrate what you've accomplished.

CONCLUSION—HOW TO DESIGN LIVE EXPERIENCES

This book offers a comprehensive exploration of how to design live experiences. Ours is a multifaceted art that goes beyond mere aesthetics. It's about creating immersive journeys that resonate with the audience, provoke change and growth, and have a lasting impact.

If you take away nothing else, consider the following eight guidelines. They present a foundational understanding of the principles involved in crafting memorable live experiences. From empathizing with the audience to designing for the bandwidth of reality, each principle contributes to the creation of compelling narratives and meaningful connections. Delve deeper into the realm of live experience design with these eight principles, and elevate your next event from ordinary to extraordinary.

EIGHT PRINCIPLES FOR DESIGNING LIVE EXPERIENCES

1. **Listen, learn, and empathize**

Open your eyes, your mind, and your heart as you explore the problems you're trying to solve. Design for the audience and add value to their lives. Put yourself in their shoes and try to figure out what matters to them. Design an experience rooted in generous, openhearted empathy that leaves them feeling understood and appreciated.

continued

2. Remember time is of the essence

Experience design isn't just volumetric or visual decisions—it's about ideas, information, and emotions. It's a dramatic experience that builds in the mind of the visitor. The most important design is the design of time. Time isn't money; it's much more valuable.

3. Design for the senses

Color changes what we feel. Sound transforms what we see. Smell determines what we taste. Synesthesia—the experience of one sense evoking and provoking another—is more common than we realize. To design for live experience, design the intersections of the senses to orchestrate symphonies of sensation.

4. Explore, experiment, and invent

Our world is so cluttered that big ideas need elbows to push things out of the way. Be brave and fearless. Don't be afraid to fail—failure is only bad if you don't learn from it. Think things that have never been thought. Ask questions that have never been asked. Design solutions that question assumptions.

5. Design for the bandwidth of reality

Live experience has the bandwidth of reality. It is a fully immersive medium. As you design the experience, design for the space that contains it or sets it free. Does the event take place in a theater with state-of-the-art AV equipment, inside a VR studio where anything is possible, or in an open field with its own challenges and opportunities? Live events bring people together in the moment. Immersive experiential design amplifies the bandwidth of reality by embracing both the constraints of the venue and its unique assets. Note: Consider the limitations and possibilities open to the virtual participant. Ambient noise and background distractions are part of the experience; plan accordingly.

6. Inspire, provoke, and connect

Your responsibility is to inspire feelings, provoke minds, affirm the reason for being here, and help people experience something they've never felt or thought before. They'll embrace what you endorse because you've established a connection that feels true.

7. Design the memories you want to create

Experience design is actually engaged in the design of thoughts, memories, and emotions. Explore, consider, and design the memories your experiences are creating. Shared memories become touchstones and building blocks upon which to construct new memories and accelerate new understandings.

8. Build a compelling narrative arc

The ultimate goal of experience design is to pull participants into a world of wonder, where challenges are met and overcome, so the individual returns in triumph, forever changed and empowered to share their newfound treasures. By initiating unexpected, perspective-altering prompts in that space, you help keep the narrative fresh, personal, and inspirational.

When you bring together the principles discussed here, you're creating moments that matter. As you look to the future, carry these principles with you. There is no limit to what you can achieve. Here's to the journey behind you, the adventure ahead, and the countless memories yet to be made.

Thanks for making us part of your journey.
We believe the work of bringing people together by
hosting live gatherings is essential to our humanity.

You are now part of this legacy.

Join our community of live event enthusiasts.

This book has served its purpose if it makes you want to seek out real-world examples of live events, talk to people who are in the industry, and compare notes regarding the latest tools, techniques, processes, and resources available to event pros.

Join our community to share and learn more about live events! We invite everyone in the vast event community to participate, and we hope to find representatives from every group.

Start here: LiveTeam.com. Don't stop.

Index

Acknowledgments

This book came together through a collaborative process that involved many people over many, many months. We are indebted to Sherry Huss and Patty Nolan for wrangling people, sources, wisdom, and words until it all made sense. We want to thank Janet Dell and the Freeman leadership team for their input and also their patience when our work disrupted theirs. We are indebted to Bruce Mau who, in his time as chief design officer, led the development of the four-phase methodology used by the Freeman team and discussed here. We want to thank those who helped inform the book's shape and content early on, including Mo Husseini and Sue Sung.

We appreciate all those who gave generously of their time during our interview and input process: Steve Anderson, Dave Arendes, Bob Audette, Mike Bruley, Bobbie Caldwell, Shana Carr, Dan Carter, Nick Catanella III, Heather Chapman, Adam Charles, Ariane Coldiron, Mike Debord, Hernan Gioiosa, Mark Fein, Paul Fletcher, Kimberley Hardcastle, Hope Hennessey, Ken Holsinger, Jay James, Mike Lamoreaux, Lou Loveland, Anytra Lowe, Rachel Mazzanti, Amanda McKillip, Mike O'Neil, Don Richards, Anemarie Roe, Jeff Rutchik, David Saef, Sachel Josefson, Chris Schimek, David Sherman, Dan Steiner, Danielle Tauber, Geb Walter, Mike Wohlitz, and Lisa Van Rosendale.

Others contributed by reading rough drafts, fact-checking, and fleshing out content: Louise Glasgow, Andrea Jensen, Hellena O'Dell, Melissa Powers, and Mickey Wilson. The Freeman marketing team developed much of the source content that is referenced here, including Martha Barnard, Amy Button, Jill Byron, John Jaeger, Geoff Kinsey, Michael Lea, and Kathe Meyers. Sherri Copes helped coordinate schedules. And Dawnn Repp, supported by Tim Mullens, managed our contracts. We are also happy to thank our partners at Greenleaf Publishers, who made straight the winding road of book publishing: Mimi Bark, Erin Brown, Haj Chenzira-Pinnock, Jen Glynn, Carrie-Sue Kay, Eleanor Fishbourne, Erin Pedigo, and Hayden Seder.

About the Authors

BOB PRIEST-HECK

Bob is known as a visionary leader of people and events. He has always worked at the forefront of innovation in the events industry, with extensive experience across business sectors, technologies, and geographies. He is respected for his progressive efforts in technology, advocacy, sustainability, and safety. Bob joined Freeman in 2011 and in 2018 became the first non–family member to serve as Freeman CEO. Bob retired from Freeman in 2024 but continues to serve on its board of directors as well as on other boards. As a champion of transformation, he is optimistic about the future of the events industry and hopes this book will encourage young people to consider a career in events as a way to provoke and lead positive change.

Bob and his wife enjoy living in the San Francisco area. They are proud of their three amazing daughters. Bob continues to blog at bphconnect.com.

CARRIE FREEMAN PARSONS

Carrie grew up in the events business and serves as chair of the board at Freeman (her grandfather is founder Buck Freeman; her father is chair emeritus Don Freeman). Carrie employs forward-thinking strategies that maintain the company's reputation as an industry innovator while staying true to its core values. Carrie has been frequently recognized by her peers and the industry at large for her outstanding contributions and achievements. As an active member of Conscious Capitalism, she's unwilling to claim success based solely on the bottom line; instead, Carrie is dedicated to leading a socially responsible organization. Just as she pushes the boundaries on what it means to create amazing brand experiences, she simultaneously provides future generations with the skills needed to make the world a better place. She hopes this book will further that effort.

Carrie lives in Dallas with her husband and is the proud mother of two exuberant young adults.